THE TOUCHSTONE
OF CHRISTIAN SINCERITY

*or The Trial of True and
False Religion*

"Saints wish to know the truth respecting themselves, whatever it may be, and no matter how difficult its attainment. Those who prefer that their supposed grace should not be tried are secretly conscious of its falseness, and of their insincerity. Reader, I do not know your case, but if your heart is in any measure right in the sight of God, you will desire to know the worst of yourself. After making the most thorough trial of which you are capable, you will be disposed to submit to the scrutiny of Him who cannot err."

John Flavel

THE TOUCHSTONE
OF CHRISTIAN SINCERITY

*or The Trial of True and
False Religion*

*"Examine yourselves, whether you are
in the faith."—2 Corinthians 13:5*

JOHN FLAVEL

1627-1691, English Puritan Preacher

2012 Edition
Edited & Updated from the 1814 Edition

Hail & Fire
www.hailandfire.com

"The Touchstone of Christian Sincerity, or The Trial of True and False Religion," by John Flavel, is herein republished from the 1814 Nathaniel Willis Edition *(entitled, "The Touchstone of Sincerity, or Trial of True and False Religion. By the Rev. John Flavel. Written anew from the original")* with edits, updates, and additional footnotes by Hail & Fire.

ISBN-10 0982804369
ISBN-13 978-0-9828043-6-0

Hail & Fire is a resource for Reformed and Gospel Theology in the works, exhortations, prayers, and apologetics of those who have maintained the Gospel and expounded upon the Scripture as the Eternal Word of God and the sole authority in Christian doctrine.

"By manifestation of the truth commending ourselves to every man's conscience in the sight of God." 2 Corinthians 4:2

www.hailandfire.com

Reseller and Bulk Order Discounts: orders@hailandfire.com

For those who hunger & thirst
after righteousness

CONTENTS

CHAPTER 1
The Lukewarm Church of Laodicea

"Because you say, 'I am rich, and increased with goods, and have need of nothing;' and do not know that you are wretched, and miserable, and poor, and blind, and naked: I counsel you to buy from me gold tried in the fire, that you may be rich."
Revelation 3:17-18

CHAPTER 1
The Lukewarm Church of Laodicea

"Because you say, 'I am rich, and increased with goods, and have need of nothing;' and do not know that you are wretched, and miserable, and poor, and blind, and naked: I counsel you to buy from me gold tried in the fire, that you may be rich."
Revelation 3:17-18

The church at Laodicea, to which these words were addressed, had degenerated much more than the other churches of Asia. The members of the Laodicean church had a name to live, but they were dead. In regard to their spiritual state, they were emphatically denominated lukewarm. They had drawn around them the form of religion, but never heartily engaged in the practice of its duties; they were strangers to its transforming efficacy, its living influence, and heavenly consolations. To this lifeless indifference, the Lord Jesus expressed his aversion: *"I would that you were cold or hot."*[1] The word cold, here, denotes the moral state of those who are wholly alienated from religion; the term hot, relates to the

---

1. Revelation 3:15.

pious temper of those who fervently love Christ and his institutions; the lukewarm, are such as have in reality too little religion to be called spiritual and yet, externally, too much the appearance of it to be esteemed carnal. The form of religion they take up as an honor or a safeguard, but the power of it they imagine would be burdensome. While they choose not to appear openly on the side of error and impiety, they are yet more unwilling to live conformably to their profession of faith. Their policy is such that they venture little, and such is their folly, that they lose all.[2]

In the text, the Laodiceans are accused of being in this deplorable state and a remedy for their spiritual malady is pointed out.

Their Moral Disease is Exposed

First, their moral disease is exposed, in its symptoms, its cause, and its aggravations.

Its symptoms are formality, indecision, listless stupidity, lukewarmness; whatever enters into the character of those professors of religion, who supremely love their temporal interests and private happiness.

Its cause is thus noted: *"You are wretched, and miserable, and poor, and blind, and naked."* All these epithets relate to the unsoundness of their

---

2. "Take heed therefore how you hear: for whosoever has, to him shall be given; and whosoever has not, from him shall be taken even that which he seems to have."—Luke 8:18.

foundation. The first two, *"wretched and miserable,"* are general, describing their condition to be lamentable, if not hopeless; the last three, *"poor, blind, naked,"* are more particular, referring to those great defects in the foundation upon which they were building, and which rendered their state so pitiable and dangerous. You are *"poor"*—devoid of righteousness and true holiness before God. These are the true riches, the riches of Christians; and he that does not possess them, is poor and miserable, however great his mental gifts or earthly treasures may be. You are *"blind"*—without Divine illumination, void of spiritual light; and so neither knowing the disease, nor the remedy; the evil of sin, or the necessity of Christ. You are *"naked"*—in a shameful, defenseless, and exposed condition, without the garments of salvation, the robe of righteousness, and the shield of faith.[3]

The aggravations of this deadly Laodicean disease, are thus stated; *"You say, I am rich, and increased with goods, and have need of nothing; but do not know,"* etc. Alas, to what absurdity and impiety does spiritual

---

3. "He has clothed me with the garments of salvation, he has covered me with the robe of righteousness."—Isaiah 61:10 | "Take unto you the whole armor of God, that you may be able to withstand in the evil day, and having done all, to stand. Stand therefore, having your loins girded about with truth, and having on the breastplate of righteousness; and your feet shod with the preparation of the Gospel of peace; above all, taking the shield of faith, wherewith you shall be able to quench all the fiery darts of the wicked. And take the helmet of salvation, and the sword of the Spirit, which is the Word of God: praying always with all prayer and supplication in the Spirit."—Ephesians 6:12-18.

delusion lead! To be destitute of holiness, without Christ, and without hope, is sufficiently distressing, but to boast of spiritual riches while in this state, is most miserable. To have the very symptoms of death upon us and yet to confidently protest that we are healthy and safe, is lamentable indeed!

A Remedy is Prescribed

Secondly, a remedy is prescribed: *"I counsel you to buy from me gold tried in the fire, that you may be rich and white raiment that you may be clothed; and anoint your eyes with eye salve that you may see."*

Let us consider what is here recommended. These metaphors represent the most superb and valuable things. Gold tried in the fire—true holiness, Christian graces that have been tried and proved. White raiment—the righteousness of the saints.[4] Eye salve—the illumination of the Holy Spirit.[5]

From where may these blessings be obtained? Buy of me, says Christ. Ordinances, ministers, angels cannot impart them to you; Christ the repository of all graces, alone, can confer them.

How are they to be acquired? Not by purchase, as those pretend, who would build a notion of merit on the words, buy of me. The exigency of the case destroys this conceit, for what can they who are

---

4. "Arrayed in fine linen, clean and white: for the fine linen is the righteousness of saints."—Revelation 19:8.

5. "When he, the Spirit of truth, is come, he will guide you into all truth."—John 16:13.

poor, and wretched, and miserable, and in need of all things, offer in payment for these divine riches?[6] Doubtless to buy, as the phrase is used here, is to cordially receive, in the ways of his own appointment, what Christ offers to freely bestow. Thus, it is elsewhere written; *"He that has no money, let him come, and buy wine and milk, without money, and without price."*[7]

Observations

In view of what has been said, then, these three observations plainly offer themselves to our consideration.

First, that many who profess faith are under very great and dangerous mistakes in regard to their character. This observation naturally arises from the scope of the text, which is to awaken and convince unsound professors.

Secondly, that true holiness is exceedingly valuable, and greatly enriches the soul, by whom it is possessed. This is suggested by the use that the Holy Spirit makes of the richest things in nature,

---

6. "They that trust in their wealth, and boast themselves in the multitude of their riches; none of them can by any means redeem his brother, nor give to God a ransom for him. For the redemption of their soul is precious."—Psalm 49:6-8 | "For there is one God, and one mediator between God and men, the man Christ Jesus."—1 Timothy 2:5.

7. Isaiah 55:1 | "For by grace are you saved through faith; and that not of yourselves: it is the gift of God. Not of works, lest any man should boast."—Ephesians 2:8-9.

to represent the unspeakable worth of Christian graces.

Thirdly, that we may safely account that only to be true holiness, which will endure all the tests appointed or permitted, for its discovery and examination. This is derived from the very significant metaphor of gold tried in the fire, by which I understand a real work of grace, manifesting and proving itself to be such, during the closest inspection and under the severest trial. For whatever puts the authenticity of one's holiness to the test, whatever scrutinizes and tries it, is to him, what fire is to gold. Hence, we read in Scripture, *"You have tried us as silver is tried,"*[8] and again, *"I will bring the third part through the fire, and will refine them as silver is refined, and try them as gold is tried."*[9]

---

8. Psalm 66:10.

9. Zechariah 13:9.

CHAPTER 2

*The Self-Deception of Many
Professed Christians*

CHAPTER 2
The Self-Deception of Many Professed Christians

Many who profess faith are under very great and dangerous mistakes in regard to their character. All flattery, and especially self-flattery, is criminal and injurious; but self-flattery, in regard to the concerns of salvation, is to the utmost degree dangerous and destructive. To pretend to goodness, which we know we do not possess, is gross hypocrisy. To persuade ourselves, or endeavor to persuade others, that we possess goodness of which we are in reality destitute, is a shameful and ruinous dissimulation. But of this, Laodiceans, and self-deceivers in every age, are guilty.

My design in these meditations is not to shake the well-founded hopes of any man or to excite unreasonable apprehensions, but to discover the radical and fatal defects in the basis of many men's expectations of future happiness. Men must judge of their religion by examining its foundation, for if that fails, the superstructure is perishable and worthless.

There is a laudable spirit of caution, cherished by the saints, which makes them sensible to the danger of self-deception, and renders them watchful and circumspect.[1] There is also a culpable anxiety and fear, tending only to gloom and despondency, to which they sometimes give way. By the former, they are guarded against evil, by the latter they incur needless grief and are restrained from inward peace.[2]

Sometimes good men, indulging groundless fears of hypocrisy, are blind to the clearest evidences of their gracious state; but more frequently, the wicked, regardless of consequences, close their eyes upon the proofs of their guilt and jeopardy. This is an evil in regard to both, but less hazardous in one case, than in the other. For he that does not see his own graces, and does not realize his privileges, does but deprive himself of quiet and enjoyment for a short time; whereas he that shuts his eyes against

---

1. "Real believers are always thinking they believe not, therefore they are fighting, wrestling, striving, and toiling without ceasing, to preserve and increase their faith. Just as good and skilful masters of any art are always seeing and observing that something is lacking in their work, whilst bunglers and pretenders persuade themselves that they lack nothing, but that all they make and do is quite perfect."—Martin Luther, *Watchwords for the Warfare of Life.*

2. "Why read over the evidences of God's love to your soul, as a man does a book which he intends to confute? Why do you study evasions, and turn off those comforts which are due to you?" | "We ought to regard what can be said in our favor, as well as what may be said against us. It is the sin of upright persons sometimes, to exercise an unreasonable severity against themselves."—John Flavel, *Keeping the Heart.*

the evidences of his sin and condemnation procures the endless destruction of his soul. Of this class of self-deceivers, the world is full, and with their case, I shall have much to say.[3]

In this chapter, I shall endeavor to make it evident, that among those who profess faith, many are deceived; to assign the causes of their deception; and to make such inferences and reflections as the subject suggests.

Evidences that Many Are False Christians
More Professed Christians than Converts

That many who profess faith are deceived is evident from the fact that there are more professed Christians than converts. There are many who profess faith who are Christians only by education—persons who have grown up in the

---

3. "The lack of distinguishing in things that appertain to experimental religion, is one of the chief miseries of the professing world. It is attended with very many most dismal consequences: multitudes of souls are fatally deluded about themselves and their own state; and so are eternally undone. Hypocrites are confirmed in their delusions, and exceedingly puffed up with pride. Many sincere Christians are dreadfully perplexed, darkened, tempted, and drawn aside from the way of duty; and sometimes sadly tainted with false religion, to the great dishonor of Christianity, and hurt of their own souls. Some of the most dangerous and pernicious enemies of religion in the world, (though they are called bright Christians,) are encouraged and honored; who ought to be discountenanced and shunned by everybody: and thus, prejudices are begotten and confirmed, in vast multitudes, against everything wherein the power and essence of godliness consists; and in the end, Deism and Atheism are promoted."—Jonathan Edwards' *Reflections on the Life of Brainard* (Styles' *Life of Brainard*).

church, but who have never been translated out of the kingdom of darkness into the kingdom of Christ. Others have been induced by the influence of custom, by slavish fears, by ambition or by more unworthy motives, to profess Christianity. Now all such deceive themselves and while they accelerate their eternal ruin, they greatly increase its aggravations. Let them reflect, that to appear, in the view of men, like Christians, is one thing, to be Christians indeed, in the sight of God, is quite another; for except a man be born of the Spirit he cannot enter the kingdom of heaven.[4]

Many Professed Christians Practice Only the Externals of Religion

Many professed Christians are acquainted only with the externals of religion and practice only an outward compliance with the commands of God. They know nothing of that inward, vital religion, which is seated in the affections of the heart, which subdues its sinful propensities and purifies its desires. But what will their external conformity avail? Or what is it but a miserable imitation of that which lives in good men and prepares them for heaven? Surely, it can have no better effect than to fit them, at last, to accuse and condemn themselves.[5]

---

4. John 3:5.

5. "If we are not in good earnest in religion and our wills and inclinations are not strongly exercised, we are nothing. The things of religion are so great, that there can be no suitableness in the exercises of our hearts, to their nature and importance, unless they are lively and powerful. In nothing is vigor in the actings of our inclinations

Certain it is, that there are many professors of this class, who, like Jehu, take no heed to walk in the way of the Lord God of Israel with their heart;[6] who deceive themselves or endeavor to deceive others, and who will sooner or later receive the fearful reward of their doings.

Professed Christians Multiply in Prosperity, but in Adversity they Fall Away

That many professed Christians are self-deluded appears from the fact that, in severe trials, large numbers fall away. Prosperity multiplies false professors, but by adversity the church is disencumbered of them; they are removed from their steadfastness, as dry leaves are carried away by a tempest.[7] *"They go out from us, that it may be made manifest that they were not of us." "When tribulation or persecution arises because of the Word, they are quickly*

---

so requisite, as in religion; and in nothing is lukewarmness so odious."—Jonathan Edwards, *Religious Affections.*

6. 2 Kings 10:31.

7. "Many profess Christianity, not because the means of grace warm the heart, or that they see any excellency in the way of God above the world, but merely to follow the fashion." | "Religion in credit makes many professors, but few proselytes; but when religion suffers, then its confessors are no more than its converts; for custom makes the former, but conscience the latter. He that is a professor of religion merely for custom-sake when it prospers, will never be a martyr for Christ's sake, when religion suffers. He that owns the truth, to live upon that, will disown it, when it comes to live upon him."—Matthew Mead, *The Almost Christian Discovered* (1661).

offended."[8] Had they been told, at first, that their professions and zeal would end in this way, their reply would probably have been like that of Hazael to the man of God: *"What, is your servant a dog, that he should do this thing?"*[9] Alas, how different is their brilliant and hopeful morning to their dark and gloomy evening! These professed believers have more of the moon than the sun; they have little light, little heat, but many changes.[10]

Many Professed Christians Indulge Secret Sins

Another proof that there are numerous false professors is that many secretly indulge some

---

8. 1 John 2:19 and Matthew 13:21.

9. 2 Kings 8:13.

10. "It is with professors of religion, especially such as become so in a time of outpouring of the Spirit of God, as it is with blossoms in the spring—there are vast numbers of them upon the trees, which all look fair and promising; yet many of them never come to anything. And many of those, that will in a little time wither up, drop off, and rot under the trees, for awhile look as beautiful and full of life as the others; and not only this, but they smell sweet and send forth a pleasant fragrance; so that we cannot, by any of our senses, positively distinguish which are those blossoms that have in them that secret virtue, which will afterwards appear in the fruit, and that inward solidity and strength which shall enable them to bear, and cause them to be perfected by the hot summer sun, that will but dry up the others. It is the mature fruit that comes afterwards, and not the beautiful color and smell of the blossoms, which we must judge by. So new converts, (professedly so,) in their talk about things of religion may appear fair, and be very savory, and the saints may think they talk feelingly. They may relish their talk, and imagine they perceive a divine savor in it, and yet all may come to nothing."—Jonathan Edwards, *Religious Affections* (1746).

beloved lust, which, like a worm at the root, cripples and kills them. Such persons may have excellent gifts and perform various and difficult duties, but pampering one lust or allowing one secret sin will destroy them. To cut off a right hand or pluck out a right eye, to deny themselves and forsake all for Christ,[11] requires such a heart religion, as they do not possess. They study to exhibit a becoming exterior deportment, they refrain from open impieties, and visibly conform to their profession, and hence they imbibe great confidence, and display themselves with much assurance; but they secretly love and practice iniquity, they cherish some known sin, and thus flatter, and deceive, and ruin their own souls.[12]

---

11. "If your right eye offends you, pluck it out, and cast it from you: for it is profitable for you that one of your members should perish, and not that your whole body should be cast into hell. And if your right hand offends you, cut it off, and cast it from you: for it is profitable for you that one of your members should perish, and not that your whole body should be cast into hell."—Matthew 5:29-30 | "Whosoever will come after me, let him deny himself, and take up his cross, and follow me. For whoever will save his life shall lose it; but whoever shall lose his life for my sake and the Gospel's, the same shall save it. For what shall it profit a man, if he shall gain the whole world, and lose his own soul? Or what shall a man give in exchange for his soul?"—Mark 8:34-37.

12. "The Scriptural representations of the state of the Christian on earth, by the images of 'a race,' and 'a warfare;' of its being necessary to rid himself of every circumstance which might retard him in the one, and to furnish himself with the whole armor of God for being victorious in the other, are, so far as these nominal Christians are concerned, figures of no propriety or meaning. As little have they, in correspondence with the Scripture descriptions of the feelings and language of real Christians, any idea of acquiring

Many Professed Christians Neglect Private Devotions

Those professors of faith, who are unaccustomed to the daily practice of secret devotion, constitute no small part of the multitude who are deceived. There are many who attend the public ordinances of religion and who either statedly or occasionally engage in social worship with the family, but whose religion does not lead them to the closet, nor incline them to any unobserved communion with heaven. These people call themselves children of God, but their piety comprises nothing so personal or particular, nothing which so much distinguishes them from the heedless world, nothing which renders the hope of salvation so interesting or the possibility of endless woe so horrible, as to give them a relish for prayer, devout meditation, and secret communion with God. They shrink from the idea of retiring by themselves and laying their hearts open to that invisible being, that holy God, whom they profess to love and worship. They contrive therefore to forget their secret sins, if not all their sins, to be unconscious of what they lack, and to impose on themselves by substituting casual outward formality, for that godliness which has the promise of the life to come. Reader, if your heart were right with God, and you did not cheat yourself with a vain profession, you would have frequent occasions

a relish, while on earth, for the worship and service of heaven. If the truth must be told, their notion is rather a confused idea of future gratification in heaven, in return for having put a restraint upon their inclinations, and endured so much religion while on earth."—William Wilberforce, *Real Christianity* (1797).

for the peculiar duties of private devotion, which you would conceal even from your most intimate friends. *"Love does not vaunt itself."*[13] True piety can, by no means, entirely lay itself open to the eyes of men; public actions and appearance may support its credit, but secret exercises must maintain its life, and supply its purest enjoyment.

Religion is not the Chief Concern of Many Professed Christians

There are, in these days, many professed Christians who never made religion their chief concern, and who, therefore, though they have a name to live, are dead in sin. While there are those who 'give themselves to the Lord;' 'whose conversation and treasure is in heaven;'[14] 'the end of whose life is Christ;'[15] who give religion the precedence both in their affections and their time; and who are constant and unwearied in the service of God; there are also those whose religion does not engross their attention, and occupies little of their

---

13. 1 Corinthians 13:4.

14. "Our conversation is in heaven; from where also we look for the Savior, the Lord Jesus Christ."—Philippians 3:20 | "For where your treasure is, there will your heart be also."—Matthew 6:21.

15. "If then, you are risen with Christ, seek those things that are above, where Christ sits at the right hand of God. Set your affection on things above, not on things on the earth. For you are dead, and your life is hid with Christ in God. When Christ, who is our life, shall appear, then shall you also appear with him in glory. Mortify therefore your members which are upon the earth; fornication, uncleanness, inordinate affection, evil concupiscence, and covetousness."—Colossians 3:1-6.

time. So far from being the chief object of their solicitude, it is treated as if anything else is more important,[16] and when they pretend to engage in it, their thoughts and hearts are somewhere else.[17] It is not their design, in attending to the duties of religion, to honor or to have fellowship with God, to become conformed to his law, to have their unholy propensities subdued, or the genuineness of their piety tried; they pray as if they prayed not, and hear as if they heard not; and if they derive no benefit from ordinances, if they acquire no animation from their discharge of duties, they are not disappointed, for they anticipated no such effects.[18]

From these considerations, it is sufficiently manifest, that many of those who profess faith deceive

---

16. "A certain man made a great supper and invited many: and sent his servant at suppertime to say to them that were invited, 'Come; for all things are now ready.' And they all with one consent began to make excuses. The first said to him, 'I have bought a piece of ground and I must go and see it: I pray you have me excused.' And another said, 'I have bought five yoke of oxen and I go to test them: I pray you have me excused.' And another said, 'I have married a wife and therefore I cannot come.'"—Luke 14:16-20.

17. "This people draws near to me with their mouth and honors me with their lips, but their heart is far from me."—Matthew 15:8.

18. "Things that are not believed, work no more upon the affections than if they had no being; and this is the grand reason why the generality of men suffer their affections to go after the world, setting the creature in the place of God in their hearts. Most men judge of the reality of things by their visibility and proximity to sense."—Matthew Mead, *The Almost Christian Discovered* (1661).

themselves in regard to their character and the reason of their hopes.

Causes of their Delusions & Dissimulation

There are four principal causes of the delusion and dissimulation of false Christians.

Deceitfulness of the Heart

First, the deceitfulness of the heart. The hearts of such men, and of all the impenitent, *are deceitful above all things, and desperately wicked.*[19] They are so full of sophistry and guile, so changeable and illusive in their operations, and so incurably and perversely inclined to evil,[20] that they will be found, at last, to have been a sufficient cause of men's ruin. The wicked, when finally cast away, will be sensible that the shame and the blame of their perdition, is ascribable wholly to themselves.[21] They will see that the self-adulation, the hypocrisy, the unbelief, the contempt of serious piety, and the bold indifference to the invitations and threatenings of God's Word, which they have practiced, were suited to prepare

---

19. Jeremiah 17:9.

20. "God saw that the wickedness of man was great in the earth, and that every imagination of the thoughts of his heart was only evil continually."—Genesis 6:5.

21. "There is none righteous, no, not one: there is none that understands, there is none that seeks after God. They are all gone out of the way, they are together become unprofitable; there is none that does good, no not one."—Romans 3:10-12.

them for endless woe. Truly, *"he that trusts in his own heart, is a fool."*[22]

Workings & Deceptions of Satan

Second, the machinations of Satan. False Christians are eminently exposed to the diabolical arts and influence of this roaming adversary;[23] they lay themselves open to his foul suggestions and, by their love of error and their fondness of sensuality, they both invite and ensure success to his studied artifice. Hence, it is not to be wondered at, that he takes them captive at his own will. He is the god of this world that blinds the minds of them that believe not,[24] and decoys the thoughtless wretches into hell; they of all men are most ready to close with his devices and yield to his impostures. With

---

22. Proverb 28:26 | "A hard heart now makes heaven and hell seem but trifles. We have showed them everlasting glory and misery, and they are as men asleep; our words are as stones cast against a wall, which fly back in our faces. We talk of terrible things, but it is to dead men; we search the wounds, but they never feel it; we speak to rocks rather than to men; the earth will as soon tremble, as they will. But when these dead souls are revived, what passionate sensibility, what working affections, what pangs of horror, what depths of sorrow will there then be! How violently will they denounce and reproach themselves! How will they rage against their former madness! The lamentations of the most affectionate wife for the loss of her husband, or of the most tender mother for the loss of her children, will be nothing to theirs for the loss of heaven."—Richard Baxter, *The Saint's Everlasting Rest.*

23. "Your adversary the devil, as a roaring lion, walks about, seeking whom he may devour."—1 Peter 5:8.

24. 2 Timothy 2:26 and 2 Corinthians 4:4.

reference to them, Basil[25] represents this apostate spirit, as insolently addressing Christ, saying: *"I have them! I have them! In spite of all your blood and miracles, your wooing and beseeching, your knocking and striving, I have cheated you of them at the very gates of heaven; notwithstanding all their illuminations and tasting of the powers of the world to come, I have wrecked them in the very mouth of the harbor."*

Deceptions of Emotion & Imagination

Third, the effects wrought in many unregenerate professors—the excitements of feeling, the raptures of fancy, the animations of hope, the bliss of ideal safety, and the pleasure of living however they wish, without obscuring their prospects or disturbing their consciences—greatly increases and confirms their delusions.[26] They do not distinguish between

---

25. 'St. Basil the Great,' 330-379 ad, Bishop of Caesarea. The writings of Basil can be found online and in such compilations as Philip Schaff's *Select Library of the Christian Church, Nicene and Post-Nicene Fathers.*

26. "The majority of souls suck nothing but delusion and presumption and hardening out of the Gospel. Many souls reason for more liberty to sin from mercy. But behold, how the Lord backs it with a dreadful word: *'who will by no means clear the guilty.'* As many as do not condemn themselves before the tribunal of justice," and "do not flee to mercy for absolution, the sentence of condemnation stands unrepealed." Oh, "how hard is it to extort any confession of guilt out of you—except in general! If we condescend to particulars, many of you will plead innocency in almost everything, though you have, like children, learned to speak these words that you are sinners. I beseech you consider it; it is no light matter, for God will by no means clear the guilty, by no means, by no entreaties, no flatteries." "He

the operations and fruits of the Spirit of God, in the sanctification of men, and the effects of error, of ignorance, of stupidity, of enthusiasm, or of diabolical influence. Their own experience is the standard by which they judge of themselves and that, not infrequently, is such as to dazzle and infatuate them. They are ready to say, *"I am rich and increased with goods, and have need of nothing."* Among those who are deceived in this way, some assume the office of religious teachers. Let them consider the words of him by whom teachers must be judged: *"Many will say to me in that day, Lord, Lord, have we not prophesied in your name—and in your name done many wonderful works?"* To whom the judge will say, *"I never knew you: depart from me."*[27]

---

will pardon all kinds of sin and absolve all manner of guilty persons—but such as do condemn themselves, such as are guilty in their own conscience and their mouths stopped before God. You who do not enter into the serious examination of your ways and do not arraign yourselves before God's tribunal daily until you find yourselves loathsome and desperate, and no refuge left for you; you who flatter yourselves always in the hope of heaven and put the fear of hell always away from you, I say, God will by no means, no prayers, no entreaties, clear or pardon you, because you come not to Jesus Christ, in whom is preached forgiveness and remission of sins. You who take liberty to sin, because God is gracious, and delay repentance until the end, because God is long-suffering, know that God will not clear you; He is holy and just as He is merciful. If his mercy does not make you fear and tremble before Him and does not separate you from your sins," "certainly you do in vain presume upon His mercy."—Hugh Binning, *Common Principles of the Christian Religion.*

27. Matthew 7:22-23 | "Be not many teachers, knowing that we shall receive the greater condemnation."—James 3:1.

Comparing Themselves Among Themselves

The practice of comparing themselves with others is a cause of deception among many who profess faith. Thus the Pharisees by trusting in themselves, that they were righteous, and despising others, kept up a high opinion of their own merit. They elevated themselves by depressing those over whom they affected a superiority. Some false Christians, mentioned by the Apostle Paul, by *"measuring themselves by themselves, and comparing themselves among themselves,"*[28] proved that they were as deluded as they were foolish. Instead of making one man or one set of men a test for the trial of another, God has established his Word as the only standard of character,[29] and by this, those who are saints indeed form an opinion of themselves.[30]

---

28. 2 Corinthians 10:12.

29. "Scripture is given by inspiration of God, and is profitable for doctrine, for reproof, for correction, for instruction in righteousness: That the man of God may be perfect."—2 Timothy 3:16-17 | "Oh how I love your law! It is my meditation all the day. You through your commandments have made me wiser than my enemies: for they are ever with me. I have more understanding than all my teachers: for your testimonies are my meditation. I understand more than the ancients, because I keep your precepts. I have refrained my feet from every evil way, that I might keep your Word. I have not departed from your judgments: for you have taught me. How sweet are your words unto my taste! Yea, sweeter than honey to my mouth! Through your precepts I get understanding: therefore I hate every false way. Your Word is a lamp unto my feet, and a light unto my path."—Psalm 119:97-105.

30. "The Word of God (is) the only rule and the perfect rule— a rule for all your actions, civil, natural, and religious; for all must

But many false Christians want a more lax and indefinite rule; they choose to compare themselves with characters that are scandalous or with such as, in some respect, are subject to reproach. They are as sharp sighted to observe other men's faults, as they are their own supposed excellencies; they contemplate the failings of others with derision, and their own doings with admiration. They bless themselves when they behold the impieties of the wicked: *"God I thank you that I am not as other men are, extortioners, unjust, adulterers;"* and when they witness actions to which they cannot condescend:

---

be done to his glory, and his Word teaches how to attain to that end. Do not let your imaginations, do not let the examples of others, do not let the preaching of men, do not let the conclusions and acts of assemblies be your rule, except inasmuch as you find them agreeing with the perfect rule of God's Holy Word. All other rules are *regulae regulatae,* they are but like publications and intimations of the rule itself. Ordinances of assemblies are but like the herald promulgation of the king's statute and law, if it varies in anything from his intention, it is not valid and binding. I beseech you, take the Scriptures for the rule of your walking or else you will wander; the Scripture is *regula regulans,* a ruling rule. If you are not acquainted with it, you must follow the opinions or the examples of other men—and what if they lead you to destruction?" "It is the great promise of the new covenant, *'You shall be all taught of God'* (Hebrews 8:11). The Scriptures can make a man learned and wise, learned to salvation." "The doctrine of Jesus Christ written on the heart is a deep profound learning and the poor, simple, rudest people may, by the Spirit's teaching, become wiser than their ancients and than their ministers." "If you would seek unto God and seek eyes opened to behold the mystery of the Word, you would become wiser than your pastors, you would learn from the Spirit to pray better, you would find the way to heaven better than they can teach you or walk in it."—Hugh Binning, *Common Principles of the Christian Religion.*

"or even as this publican,"[31] Oh what a saint am I, in comparison with these creatures! A Christian may and ought to praise God that he has been made, by grace, to differ from some other men, but he cannot rake together the enormities of the worst characters, or the infirmities of the best, in order to justify and applaud himself, as these pharisaical deceivers do.[32]

Such are some of the causes of that general delusion and imposture, under which so great a portion of the professing Christian world bow down and perish.

Do Not Conclude all Christians are False

I shall now endeavor to improve this topic, as briefly and with as much closeness of application, as its importance and copiousness will admit.

Let me caution you to beware of inferring from what has been said, that all those who profess faith are deceivers of both themselves and others, and that there is no truth or integrity in any man. This

---

31. Luke 18:11.

32. "He that is under the influence of this distemper (of spiritual pride), is apt to think highly of his attainments in religion, as comparing himself with others. It is natural for him to fall into that thought of himself, that he is an eminent saint, that he is very high among the saints, and has distinguishingly good and great experiences." "Hence such are apt to put themselves forward among God's people." "But he whose heart is under the power of Christian humility, is of a contrary disposition."—Jonathan Edwards, *Religious Affections.*

would be to affect the prerogative of God with intolerable arrogance and to judge the hearts of men with desperate severity.

Some men are as apt to conclude that those are hypocrites, whose hearts they measure by their own,[33] as others are to decide that they themselves are saints, by comparing their fancied virtues with the vices and crimes of the most abandoned. But blessed be God there is some grain amidst the heaps of chaff and rubbish: the devil does not have the entire portion; a remnant, according to election, is truly and exclusively the Lord's.

Let none imagine, because so many professing Christians are sorely deceived, that assurance is unattainable. It is indeed one of the rarest and most difficult acquisitions, but it is far from impracticable. Hence, all are commanded to *"give diligence to make their calling and election sure."*[34]

I warn you not to conceal the truths of God or the graces of his Spirit, nor to be deterred from openly

---

33. "Many hunt down those sins in others which they gladly shelter in themselves."—Charles Spurgeon, *Feathers for Arrows*.

34. 2 Peter 1:10 | "Assurance is not so much to be obtained by self examination as by action. The Apostle Paul sought assurance chiefly this way, even by *forgetting the things that were behind, and reaching forward unto those that were before, pressing towards the mark for the prize of the high calling of God in Christ Jesus; if by any means he might attain unto the resurrection of the dead.'* And it was by this means, chiefly, that he obtained assurance, *'I therefore so run, not as uncertainly.'* He obtained assurance of winning the prize, more by running, than by considering."—Jonathan Edwards, *Religious Affections*.

professing them, because many deceive themselves and others by a vain profession. Should you hide what you have, because another pretends to what he has not? The possession of holiness in your own soul is indeed what secures you from perdition, but the profession of it is what honors God, edifies the saints, and sometimes awakens sinners.[35] Vain and ambitious display is sinful, but a serious and humble profession is an unquestionable duty.[36]

Do Not Be High Minded, But Fear

Having guarded what has been said from abuse, I hasten to a more direct and special improvement of the subject. Surely, I cannot better accomplish this, nor more faithfully serve you, my readers, than by warning you to see to your own soul, that

---

35. "No man, when he has lit a candle, covers it with a vessel, or puts it under a bed; but sets it on a candlestick, that those who enter in may see the light."—Luke 8:16 | "Faith comes by hearing, and hearing by the Word of God."—Romans 10:17 | "Go into all the world and preach the Gospel to every creature. He that believes and is baptized shall be saved; but he that does not believes shall be damned."—Mark 16:15-16 | "It pleased God by the foolishness of preaching to save them that believe."—1 Corinthians 1:20-21.

36. "If we live in the Spirit, let us also walk in the Spirit. Let us not be desirous of vain glory, provoking one another, envying one another."—Galatians 5:25-26 | "Be an example of the believers, in word, in conversation, in love, in spirit, in faith, in purity. Until I come, give attention to reading, to exhortation, to doctrine. Do not neglect the gift that is in you." "Meditate on these things; give yourself wholly to them; that your profiting may appear to all. Take heed to yourself, and to the doctrine; continue in them: for in doing this you will save both yourself, and them that hear you."—1 Timothy 4:12-16.

you might not be among the number who deceive themselves. Permit me then to press that great Apostolic caution, *"Let him that thinks he stands, take heed lest he fall."*[37] Oh professed believers, look carefully to your foundation; do not be high minded but fear.[38] You may have done and suffered many things for religion's sake, you may have excellent gifts and great comforts, much zeal for God and high confidence in your integrity—and all this may be right, but it may possibly be counterfeit and vain. Perhaps you have sometimes, upon examination, pronounced yourselves upright, but remember that the Searcher of hearts has not yet delivered his final sentence. If he weighs you in the balance of truth and finds you lacking, how greatly you will be confounded and dismayed! Saints may look upon you with approbation, but they do not see as God sees; you may have a name to live, while dead.

You know the fate of the apostate professors mentioned in the Gospel—take heed that their case is not your own. Do they not all cry to you with one voice: "If you would not come where we are, do not flatter yourselves as we did; if you expect a better portion, be sure you get a better heart. If we had been more suspicious of ourselves, we would have been much safer."[39]

---

37. 1 Corinthians 10:12.

38. Romans 11:20.

39. In *The Pilgrim's Progress,* John Bunyan gives the following description of apostasy and despair in the dialogue between

I would not frighten you with groundless alarms, but I would gladly prevent fatal mistakes. Do you not find your hearts deceitful in many things? Do you not shuffle over secret duties? Do you not condemn in others, evils that you scarcely reprove in yourselves? Are there not many selfish ends in your performances? Do you not find that you are far less affected with a great deal of service, done for God, by others, than with a little service done by yourselves? Is it not hard for you to look, without envy, upon the excellencies of other men or without pride, upon your own? Are you not troubled by a busy devil, as well as by a bad heart? Has not he that circuits the whole world observed you? Has he not studied your constitutional failings

---

Christian and the Man in an iron cage:

"Christian said to the man, What are you? The man answered, I am what I was not once.

Christian: What were you once?

Man: I was once a fair and flourishing professor, both in my own eyes, and also in the eyes of others: I was once, as I thought, fair for the Celestial City, and had then joy even at the thoughts that I should get there.

Christian: Well but what are you now?

Man: I am now a man of despair and am shut up in it as in this iron cage. I cannot get out. Oh now I cannot!

Christian: But how did you come to this condition?

Man: I did not watch and be sober: I laid the reins upon the neck of my lusts; I sinned against the light of the Word, and the goodness of God; I have grieved the Spirit, and he is gone; I tempted the devil and he is come to me; I have provoked God to anger, and he has left me; I have so hardened my heart, that I cannot repent."

and discovered the sin that most easily overtakes you? Has he less wrath towards your souls, than towards those around you? Surely, you are in the very thicket of temptations; thousands of snares are on every side. Alas! How few of the professing and anticipating world win heaven in the end. How hard it is to be upright, with what difficulty are even the righteous saved![40] Therefore search your hearts and may this caution penetrate your inmost souls: *"Let him that thinks he stands, take heed lest he fall."* Away with such uncharitable censuring of others and be more just and severe in rebuking yourselves. Away with unprofitable controversies, spend your thoughts, rather, upon this momentous question, "Am I sound or am I rotten at heart?" "Am I a new creature or the old disguised in borrowed clothing?"[41] Let it be your earnest prayer, that you may not be deceived in this point. Pray and labor that you may not be given up to a heedless and

---

40. 1 Peter 4:18.

41. "If any man be in Christ, he is a new creature: old things are passed away; behold, all things are become new."—2 Corinthians 5:17 | "Mortify therefore your members which are upon the earth; fornication, uncleanness, inordinate affection, evil concupiscence, and covetousness, which is idolatry: for which things' sake the wrath of God comes on the children of disobedience: In the which you also walked some time, when you lived in them. But now you also put off all these; anger, wrath, malice, blasphemy, filthy communication out of your mouth. Do not lie to one another, seeing that you have put off the old man with his deeds; and have put on the new man."—Colossians 3:5-10.

vain spirit, having religious duties as a rattle, only to beguile and hush your consciences.[42]

Surely, that groundwork upon which your hope for eternal life is built cannot be too carefully or safely laid down. I dare promise you, that when you come to die, you will not regret having devoted much time and attention to this matter. While others, then, are panting after the dust of the earth and crying *"who will show us any good,"* may you be endeavoring after the assurance of the love of God, and seeking to make your calling and election sure.

Do not deceive yourselves with names and notions; they cannot change your heart. If you are still impenitent, if you have not been renewed and

---

42. Concerning the falling away of hypocrites, John Bunyan says, "They draw away their thoughts, all that they can, from the remembrance of God, death, and the judgment to come. Then, by degrees, they cast off private duties, such as private prayer, curbing their lusts, watching, sorrow for sin, and the like. Then they shun the company of lively and warm Christians. After that, they grow cold to public duties, such as hearing, reading, godly conference, and the like. Then they begin to pick holes, as we say, in the coats of some of the godly, and that devilishly; that they may have a seeming reason to throw religion behind their backs, for the sake of some infirmity they have spied in them. Then they begin to adhere to and associate themselves with carnal, loose, and wanton men. Then they cut loose in carnal and wanton discourses in secret, and are glad if they can see such things in any that are accounted honest, that they may the more boldly do it through their example. After this, they begin to play with little sins openly, and then, being hardened, they show themselves as they are. Thus being launched again into the gulf of misery, unless a miracle of grace prevent it, they perish everlastingly in their own deceptions."—*The Pilgrim's Progress.*

sanctified by the Spirit of God, it matters little by what name you are called, or how warmly you advocate the distinguishing doctrines of the Gospel—you are in the sight of God a guilty, perishing sinner.

Once more, my friends, I warn you to examine the foundation upon which you rest: do not deceive yourselves; behold, the Judge, who knows your works, stands at the door.[43]

Concluding Thoughts

To conclude: if, as we have reason to believe, a great many of those who profess faith, and others whose hopes are no less confident, are fatally deceived, then it becomes those, who have good reason to believe that they are indeed the children of God, to praise and glorify him for his mercy, as long as they live. There are doubtless many real Christians, who do not themselves perceive such evidence of their gracious state, as to fully satisfy themselves:[44] but let them not be discouraged; let them resolutely persevere and constantly live as the grace of God teaches.[45] And let such as have daily,

---

43. James 5:9 | "Shall God not search this out? For he knows the secrets of the heart."—Psalm 44:21.

44. "If our heart condemn us, God is greater than our heart, and knows all things."—1 John 3:20.

45. "Do not turn aside from following the Lord, but serve the Lord with all your heart; and do not turn aside: for then you would go after vain things, which cannot profit or deliver."—1 Samuel 12:20-22 | "Whatever be the ground of one's distress, it should drive him to, not from God."—John Flavel, *Keeping the Heart.*

unequivocal evidence of their sanctification, freely enjoy the elevated happiness, and the transporting anticipations, peculiar to their state of mind.[46]

---

46. "If our heart does not condemn us, then we have confidence toward God. And whatsoever we ask, we receive of him, because we keep his commandments, and do those things that are pleasing in his sight. And this is his commandment, That we should believe on the name of his Son Jesus Christ, and love one another, as he gave us commandment. And he who keeps his commandments dwells in him, and he in him. And hereby we know that he abides in us, by the Spirit which he has given us."—1 John 3:21-24 | "Rejoice in the Lord always: and again I say, rejoice."—Philippians 4:4.

CHAPTER 3
*The Exceeding Value of True Holiness
or Saving Grace*

CHAPTER 3
The Exceeding Value of True Holiness
or Saving Grace

Holiness, or saving grace, is exceedingly valuable and greatly enriches those who possess it.

Evidences of its Exceeding Value

To represent saving grace or true holiness, our Lord employs terms relating to the most pure, valuable, and magnificent things within the treasures of nature—and surely that which can only be faintly shadowed by the richest of natural objects, must be the greatest moral good.

We may easily satisfy ourselves that the value of saving grace is not to be described or conceived, by the following several considerations.

First: if we consider saving grace in respect to its cause, we shall find that it is a peculiar work or fruit of the divine Spirit; the Spirit, on this account, is called *"the Spirit of grace"* and *"the Spirit of holiness."*[1] All the rules of morality, with all possible human diligence and effort—*alone*—can never produce one

---

1. Zechariah 12:10 and Romans 1:4.

gracious act or one holy exercise.[2] Such, indeed, is the incomparable worth of efficacious grace, that all other gifts of the Spirit are represented in Scripture as comparatively worthless.

Second: the very nature of saving grace implies its unspeakable value. It is that by which the saints are made to resemble God in moral beauty and goodness; it is that which renders them objects of the Divine complacency and fits them to glorify and enjoy their Creator and Redeemer forever.

Third: saving grace appears peculiarly excellent if we reflect that it is bestowed only upon those whom God has elected to everlasting life.[3] It is not,

2. *"'I am the vine,' says he, 'you are the branches. My Father is the husbandman. As the branch cannot bear fruit of itself, except it abide in the vine, no more can you, except you abide in me. For without me you can do nothing.'* John 15:1 and 4-5. If we cannot bear fruit of ourselves, anymore than a branch can bud after it is torn up from the ground, and deprived of moisture, we must no longer seek for any aptitude in our nature to that which is good. There is no ambiguity in this conclusion, *'Without me you can do nothing.'* He does not say that we are too weak to be sufficient for ourselves, but reducing us to nothing, excludes every idea of ability, however diminutive."—John Calvin, *Institutes of the Christian Religion.*

3. Scripture teaches us that God made *'man upright; but they sought out many inventions,'* that, *"all have sinned, and come short of the glory of God,"* and that, *"there is none righteous, no, not one: there is none that understands, there is none that seeks after God,"* (Ecclesiastes 7:29, Romans 3:23 & 10-12; and also Psalm 58:3 & James 1:13-15). Hence, all mankind has justly merited eternal condemnation: *"for the wages of sin is death,"* (Romans 6:23). Yet, it has pleased God to draw unto himself (John 6:44), and sanctify unto himself, an elect remnant: *"as it is written, Jacob have I loved, but Esau have I hated. What shall we say then? Is there*

like many other gifts, made common to all, but is imparted only to those who are chosen in Christ Jesus[4] and made heirs of glory.

Fourth: the influence and fruits of saving grace in the souls of saints proclaim its unspeakable worth—for it elevates and ennobles, adorns and beautifies the soul, it raises the affections to heaven, employs them upon divine objects, and transforms the heart into the image of God; it preserves the saints from known and allowed iniquities, so that although sin still works in them, it cannot bring forth fruit unto death. It establishes them, in faith and peace, on the Rock of Ages, from which they shall never be removed; and it is the root of all the fruit which they bring forth to God in this world—of every gracious word on their lips, and

---

unrighteousness with God? God forbid. For he says to Moses, I will have mercy on whom I will have mercy, and I will have compassion on whom I will have compassion. So then it is not of him that wills, nor of him that runs, but of God that shows mercy." For, *"he loved us, even when we were dead in sins,"* (Ephesians 2:4-5) and sent the Savior, Jesus Christ, to redeem his elect. *"Therefore he has mercy on whom he will have mercy, and whom he will he hardens. You will say then to me, Why does he yet find fault? For who has resisted his will? Nay but, Oh man, who are you that replies against God? Shall the thing formed say to him that formed it, Why have you made me thus? Has not the potter power over the clay, of the same lump to make one vessel unto honor, and another unto dishonor?"* (Romans 9:11-24).

4. "You have not chosen me, but I have chosen you."—John 15:16 | "God has from the beginning chosen you to salvation through sanctification of the Spirit and belief of the truth."—2 Thessalonians 2:13 | "For by grace are you saved through faith; and that not of yourselves: it is the gift of God: not of works, lest any man should boast."—Ephesians 2:8-9.

every gracious work in their hands.[5] Be the substance of their good thoughts, their heavenly discourses, and holy prayers never so excellent, grace is the root and source of them all.

Fifth: the exceeding value of saving grace will appear if we further consider its properties. As has already been observed, the most expressive epithets are employed to describe it; I may add that it is unfailing and immortal. It is as a well of water, springing up unto everlasting life.[6] It will not fail and perish with your mortal body, but will ascend to glory with your soul, from which it is inseparable. You may outlive your friends, your estates, and whatever else you now possess, but if you have true holiness, it will endure as long as you exist.[7]

---

5. "Working in you that which is well pleasing in his sight, through Jesus Christ."—Hebrews 13:21 | "For it is God which works in you both to will and to do."—Philippians 2:13 | "For I will take you from among the heathen, and gather you out of all countries, and will bring you into your own land. Then will I sprinkle clean water upon you, and you shall be clean: from all your filthiness, and from all your idols, will I cleanse you. A new heart also will I give you, and a new Spirit will I put within you: and I will take away the stony heart out of your flesh, and I will give you a heart of flesh. And I will put my Spirit within you, and cause you to walk in my statutes, and you shall keep my judgments, and do them."—Ezekiel 36:24-27.

6. "Whoever drinks of the water that I shall give him shall never thirst; but the water that I shall give him shall be in him a well of water springing up into everlasting life."—John 4:14.

7. "Holiness becomes your house, Oh Lord, forever."—Psalm 93:5 | "For the Lord God gives them light: and they shall reign forever and ever."—Revelation 22:5 | "Being made free from sin, and become servants to God, you have your fruit unto holiness,

Sixth: nor is the value of saving grace any less conspicuous in the design with which it is wrought in us by the Holy Spirit, that is: to purify us from all iniquity, to free us from imperfection, and to render us fit for the heavenly inheritance—for the service and enjoyment of God in the world above.[8]

Seventh: the means that are adapted to procure the dispensation of grace to men, and those employed in producing and preserving holiness in the saints, are conclusive evidences of its infinite worth. The incarnation, the sufferings, and the intercession of Jesus Christ, were necessary to prepare the Way; the special agency of the Holy Spirit, is necessary to produce the effect. The ordinances and institutions of the Gospel were first appointed and have been continued, in order that holiness might be produced and preserved in the hearts of saints; not only that, but even the ordinary dispensations of Providence are designed, in some way, to subserve this purpose.

Eighth: the peculiar regard that is vouchsafed by the Most High, to every degree, every exercise, and

---

and the end everlasting life."—Romans 6:22 | "For the truth's sake, which dwells in us, and shall be with us forever."—2 John 1:2.

8. Jesus Christ "gave himself for us, that he might redeem us from all iniquity, and purify unto himself a peculiar people, zealous for good works;" "that he might sanctify and cleanse (us) with the washing of water by the Word, that he might present (us) to himself a glorious church, not having spot, or wrinkle, or any such thing; but that (we) should be holy and without blemish." (Titus 2:13-14 and Ephesians 5:25-27).

every fruit of holiness in his people, demonstrates its unspeakable importance and worth. For he who made the jewel, best knows its value.

Ninth: that holiness is a most excellent and desirable thing, is shown by the hypocritical pretences made to it all over the professing world.[9] If it did not confer some singular advantage, why should everyone pant for the reputation of possessing it? But so it is that the devil himself conceals many of his lures and hooks of temptation with a show of grace. Knowing, as he does, that sin has nothing beautiful or winning in itself, by which it can entice, he disguises it under a pretence of goodness. Let hypocrites and self-deceivers consider what they will answer at last, when it is demanded, "If grace were evil, why did you so pretend to the reputation of it? If good, why did you content yourself with the mere empty name of it?"

Tenth: in a word, the incomparable value of saving grace is manifested by the esteem that all good men have for it. Holiness is the sum of all their prayers,[10] the scope of all their endeavors, the

---

9. "As it is a great proof of the baseness and filthiness of sin, that sinners seek to cover it; so it is a great proof of the excellency of godliness, that so many pretend to it. The very hypocrite's fair profession pleads the cause of religion."—Matthew Mead, *The Almost Christian Discovered.*

10. "Lead us not into temptation, but deliver us from evil."—Matthew 6:13 | "Incline not my heart to any evil thing, to practice wicked works with men that work iniquity: and let me not eat of their delicacies."—Psalm 141:4 | "Blessed are they which do hunger and thirst after righteousness: for they shall be

substance of their joys, the relief of their afflictions and sufferings; it constitutes their riches and their glory.

Perfect Holiness in the Fear of God

Is saving grace thus valuable and precious? Beware, you who possess it, lest your hearts should be elated with spiritual pride. You have need often to reflect upon your former state of sin and condemnation, and upon your present ill-deserving and imperfection; to consider how and by whom you have been made to differ from them that perish; to ask what you have that you have not received; to feel your weakness, your dependence, and your obligations; and to remember that it is the nature of holiness to render men humble and lowly, in heart and life.[11]

---

filled."—Matthew 5:6 | "Your law is my delight."—Psalm 119:174.

11. "The very design of the Gospel tends to self-abasing; and the work of grace is begun and carried on in humiliation. Humility is not a mere ornament of a Christian, but an essential part of the new creature—it is a contradiction to be a sanctified man, or a true Christian, and not humble."—Richard Baxter, *The Reformed Pastor.*

"An infallible sign of spiritual pride is, persons being apt to think highly of their humility. False experiences are commonly attended with a counterfeit humility and it is the very nature of a counterfeit humility to be highly conceited of itself. False religious affections generally have the tendency, especially when raised to a great height, to make persons think that their humility is great, and accordingly to take much notice of their great attainments in this respect and admire them. But eminently gracious affections, (I do not scruple to say it,) are evermore of a contrary tendency, and universally have a contrary effect in those that have them. They indeed make them very sensible, what reason there is that

Is holiness more excellent than gold? Well then may the poorest Christians content themselves with the allotments of Providence. You who are destitute of this world's goods, but rich in faith and heirs of the kingdom that God has promised; you who feel the rigors of temporal poverty, but who have treasures in heaven, think of your imperishable wealth and neither thirst for an earthly portion, nor murmur at temporary wants.[12] Alas! Thousands who are penniless and thousands who have worldly wealth are without Christ and so, without hope.

If holiness is thus valuable, then those Christians who suffer it to decline or who do not grow in grace, incur such a loss as all this world's goods are not sufficient to repair.

---

they should be deeply humbled, and cause them to earnestly thirst and long after it; but they make their present humility, or that which they have already attained to, appear small; and their remaining pride, great, and exceedingly abominable."—Jonathan Edwards, *Religious Affections*.

12. "Consider that the trials and troubles, the calamities and miseries, the crosses and losses that you meet with in this world are all the hell that you shall ever have." "This is the worst of your condition, the best is to come. Lazarus had his hell first, his heaven last; but the rich man had his heaven first and his hell at last, Luk. 16:19-25.""You have all your pangs and pains and throes here that ever you shall have; your ease and rest and pleasure is to come. 'Blessed be ye poor: for yours is the kingdom of God. Blessed are ye that hunger now: for ye shall be filled. Blessed are ye that weep now: for ye shall laugh,' Luk. 6:20-21. Here you have all your bitter, your sweet is to come."—Thomas Brooks, *The Mute Christian under the Smarting Rod* (2011 Edition).

If holiness is of such worth and importance, then the ordinances and institutions of Christian religion and all the means adapted to preserve and increase it, ought to be highly esteemed and diligently employed.

If saving grace is so excellent, then it becomes saints to be peculiarly watchful and circumspect in times of degeneracy and temptation. We have read of Christians who resisted unto blood, striving against sin—who chose to part with their lives, rather than relax in their piety:[13] if we would endure unto the end, we must follow their example.[14] We live in an age of deception and temptation. Many seeming Christians have fallen and lost all, and many real Christians have lost so much, that instead of again enjoying the comforts of piety in this world, they are likely to go to the grave, repeating

13. "Therefore seeing we also are compassed about with so great a cloud of witnesses, let us lay aside every weight, and the sin which so easily besets us, and let us run with patience the race that is set before us, looking unto Jesus the author and finisher of our faith; who for the joy that was set before him endured the cross, despising the shame, and is set down at the right hand of the throne of God. For consider him that endured such contradiction of sinners against himself, lest you be wearied and faint in your minds. You have not yet resisted unto blood, striving against sin."—Hebrews 12:1-4.

14. "Take, my brethren, the prophets, who have spoken in the name of the Lord, for an example of suffering affliction, and of patience. Behold, we count them happy which endure. You have heard of the patience of Job, and have seen the end of the Lord; that the Lord full of pity and of tender mercy."—James 5:10-11.

the lamentation of Job: *"Oh that it were with me as in months past!"*[15]

Let me urge and entreat you to make it the great business of your life and the chief concern of every day, to grow in grace and to perfect holiness in the fear of God. Cultivate every advantage of time and place; improve the society of God's people,[16] and let your closets testify that your love of holiness is stronger than death.[17]

---

15. Job 29:2.

16. "Having therefore these promises, dearly beloved, let us cleanse ourselves from all filthiness of the flesh and spirit, perfecting holiness in the fear of God."—2 Corinthians 7:1 | "Awake you who sleep, and arise from the dead, and Christ shall give you light. See then that you walk circumspectly, not as fools, but as wise, Redeeming the time, because the days are evil."—Ephesians 5:14-17 | "Exhort one another daily, while it is called Today; lest any of you be hardened through the deceitfulness of sin."—Hebrews 3:12-14.

17. "Be an example of the believers, in word, in conversation, in love, in spirit, in faith, in purity." "Give attendance to reading, to exhortation, to doctrine. Do not neglect the gift that is in you." "Meditate on these things; give yourself wholly to them; that your profiting may appear to all. Take heed to yourself, and to the doctrine; continue in them: for in doing this you will both save yourself, and them that hear you."—1 Timothy 4:12-16.

CHAPTER 4

True Holiness or Saving Grace
Endures All Tests

CHAPTER 4
True Holiness or Saving Grace
Endures All Tests

We may safely account that only to be true holiness, which will endure all the tests appointed or permitted for its discovery and examination.

Trials of Men's Graces or Religious Affections

In this world it has pleased God to place all his people in a state of trial—he first tries, then crowns them.[1] No man can determine whether his graces are true or false, until they are examined by something which, to them, shall be what fire is to gold. The deceived Laodiceans imagined themselves to be rich in grace, but they proved to be wretchedly poor. For this reason, Christ counsels them to buy from him gold tried in the fire, that is, true holiness, which should endure the severest scrutiny.

The Scriptures plainly recognize a trial of men's opinions, as well as a trial of their graces; but concerning the trial of men's opinions, I shall

---

1. "Blessed is the man that endures temptation: for when he is tried, he shall receive the crown of life, which the Lord has promised to them that love him."—James 1:12.

have occasion to say but little. Doubtless, they may endanger and obstruct their salvation, by unscriptural sentiments; yet, if they have holiness of heart, notwithstanding some false opinions, *"they shall be saved, though it be as by fire:"*[2] but if they are devoid of holiness,[3] the most correct speculation will avail them nothing; they will perish and perish without remedy.

The trial of a man's graces, or religious affections, is all-important—as they are, so is his safety and happiness, and so, his prospect for eternity.

This trial may be considered in two respects:

First: as it is to be performed by ourselves; *"Examine yourselves whether you are in the faith, prove your own selves"*[4]—scrutinize your hearts in the light of divine truth; ascertain and demonstrate whether your affections are holy.

---

2. "For other foundation can no man lay than that is laid, which is Jesus Christ. Now if any man build upon this foundation gold, silver, precious stones, wood, hay, stubble; every man's work shall be made manifest: for the day shall declare it, because it shall be revealed by fire; and the fire shall try every man's work of what sort it is. If any man's work abide which he has built thereupon, he shall receive a reward. If any man's work shall be burned, he shall suffer loss: but he himself shall be saved; yet so as by fire."—1 Corinthians 3:11-15.

3. "Holiness, without which no man shall see the Lord."—Hebrews 12:14 | "Be doers of the Word, and not hearers only, deceiving your own selves."—James 1:22 | "Not with eye service, as men pleasers; but as the servants of Christ, doing the will of God from the heart."—Ephesians 6:6.

4. 2 Corinthians 13:5.

Second: as it is executed by Him *"who searches the heart, and judges according to truth."*[5]

With a view to both these kinds of trial, but especially the first, I propose in this treatise, first, to show what tries the genuineness of Christian graces, as fire tries gold; second, to exhibit the ends for which God appoints such trials of the holiness of his people, in this world; third, to prove that such only is true holiness, as will bear these trials; and fourth, to improve and apply the whole.

Signs & Tests of Christian Character

Before I enter into particulars, it seems needful to observe, that the subject to which we are approaching, is full of difficulties. Without much cautious discrimination and solicitude, with regard to the various and dissimilar capacities, attainments and circumstances, of different Christians, one could hope to do little else but confuse and mislead. Nor is less care necessary in the application of tests or signs; they should be well examined and approved before we try ourselves or others by them.[6]

---

5. "I the Lord search the heart, I try the reins, even to give every man according to his ways, and according to the fruit of his doings."—Jeremiah 17:10.

6. "It is strange how hard it is to bring men to be content with the rules and directions Christ has given them; they must go by other rules of their own inventing, which seem wiser and better to them. I know of no directions or counsels that Christ ever delivered more plainly, than the rules he has given us to guide us in judging the sincerity of others, viz, that we should judge of the tree, chiefly by the fruit. Yet this will not do; other ways

Signs or tests of character are, by some, distinguished as exclusive, inclusive, and positive. Exclusive marks serve to shut out bold pretenders, by showing them that they are utterly devoid of a saving work of grace. These are commonly taken from some indispensable ordinary duty, such as praying or hearing; which men may indeed perform and yet have no degree of holiness, but the neglect of which demonstrates a total absence of any work of grace.

Inclusive marks serve to discover the degree, rather than the existence, of holiness and are intended for comfort rather than conviction. If we perceive them in ourselves, we shall find not only real, but eminent piety; as they arise from the higher exercises of grace in confirmed and mature Christians.

Between these, there are marks or evidences called positive, which are always found in those, and those only, who have been regenerated. In the application of these, great care is requisite, since they relate as much to the feeblest Christian, as they do to the most advanced Christian. It is especially necessary to beware of representing the particular exercises or experience of those who are esteemed eminent in knowledge and grace, as a rule for those whose attainments are small.[7] This

are sought out, which are imagined to be more distinguishing and certain. Woeful have the mischievous consequences been of this arrogant setting up of men's wisdom above the wisdom of Christ."—Jonathan Edwards, *Religious Affections*.

7. "I concluded, a little grace, a little love, a little of the true fear of God, is better than all the gifts: yes, and I am fully convinced

practice is justly reprobated for its absurdity and its injurious effects.

These things being premised, I will now proceed to show what things in particular, try the temper and state of our souls—*"What tries the genuineness of Christian graces, as fire tries gold."*

It is true that all the circumstances of our lives, and every event that relates to us, may make some discovery of our hearts; yet, some limits must be prescribed to this. I shall therefore show, in the following order, what trials are made of our graces by prosperity and adversity, by our inward corruptions, by our active duties, and, lastly, by our sufferings on account of religion.

Trials of Worldly Prosperity

Prosperity, worldly success, outward enjoyments, riches, and honors—try men's hearts and reveal their thoughts. Some may fancy the fire of prosperity to be designed rather for comfort than for trial, rather to compose us, than to search us out; but scarcely anything more clearly demonstrates the falseness or soundness of one's faith.[8] It is to grace, what fire

of it, that it is possible for souls that can scarce give a man an answer, but with great confusion as to method; I say, it is possible for them to have a thousand times more grace, and so to be more in the love and favor of the Lord, than some who by the virtue of the gift of knowledge, can deliver themselves like angels."—John Bunyan, *Grace Abounding to the Chief of Sinners.*

8. "Then Jesus said to his disciples, 'Truly I say to you, that a rich man shall hardly enter into the kingdom of heaven. And

is to gold. Particularly, it occasions an exhibition of the self-flattery and delusion of those who have had a name to live, while dead, and of the unequivocal evidences of true religion, in real saints.

Trials of Prosperity on the Ungodly

Among the proofs thus exhibited, of dissimulation and deceit, are the following:

1. Prosperity occasions, in some men, a stupid forgetfulness of God and a neglect of the duties of religion. They fall asleep in the lap of abundance and do not dream that there is a God to be served and a soul to be saved. Their carnal pleasures and enjoyments, and the care of their earthly affairs, leave no time for prayers, or for reflections concerning death and eternity. Like Herod, they are lifted up with conceits of their own greatness and importance; and, like him, they mock the supremacy of Jehovah or contemn his authority, instead of obeying his commands.[9] They are so preoccupied with serving and gratifying themselves, that they usually lose those faint appearances of piety, which, in other circumstances, they might have exhibited.

2. Prosperity, meeting with one who is graceless, engrosses his thoughts and affections, and

---

again I say to you, it is easier for a camel to go through the eye of a needle, than for a rich man to enter into the kingdom of God."—Matthew 19:23-24.

9. Acts 12:21-23.

makes him wholly sensual. Earthly things have a tendency to transform men's hearts into their own similitude—to assimilate them to their nature; and they produce their full effect upon those whose faith is a mere pretence. Such, in times of prosperity—when temptations are presented and the means of indulgence within reach—will abandon themselves to sensual gratifications and show to the world the depravity of their hearts and the dissoluteness of their character. It is true that prosperity may have a very unhappy influence on the minds of good men also, but it can never produce in them such effects as have been mentioned. The allurements of forbidden objects and the enticements of sin will be counteracted by the principles, the habits, and the feelings of genuine piety. Some, indeed, although confessedly destitute of true religion and surrounded by all the facilities and incitements to sensuality which prosperity can confer, are yet, in their exterior behavior, strictly moderate and regular. Perhaps those men, who, in ordinary circumstances, make a false show of religion, are most likely to be carried off down the stream of sensuality, when prosperity suddenly attends them, but all who are affected in this way by prosperous circumstances, are evidently graceless.

3. Mere pretenders to religion, self-deceivers, and dissemblers, are apt, when prosperity surrounds them, not only to lose all concern for their own salvation, but to harden themselves against the judgments of God and the calamities and suffering

that his people endure. Instances of this kind are but too common, and they designate characters, which cannot be mistaken.

Such are some of the ways in which prosperity operates upon those who do not have true faith. Without elaborating any more minutely upon this part of the subject, I will now proceed to show the influence of prosperity on the people of God.

Trials of Prosperity on the Godly

That the saints sometimes fall into temptation, cannot be denied, and doubtless the trial of prosperity often discovers in them the workings of sin, but its general influence upon the children of God, is such as to render their graces more conspicuous, and their uprightness more certain.

1. A real saint, when prosperity and abundance flows around him, will earnestly endeavor to suppress any workings of pride, and to preserve humility and lowliness in his heart and life. I do not say that every child of God under prosperity, will at all times feel and manifest the same degree of humility, but I am sure, that there is within every one of them, that which, when thus tried, will check and allay the risings of vanity and ambition.[10] God's people have seen, and still see, too much of their own hearts, too much of this world, and

---

10. "The comforts of the true saints increase awakening and caution, and a lively sense of how great a thing it is to appear before an infinitely holy, just, and omniscient Judge."—Jonathan Edwards, *Religious Affections.*

too much of the divine excellence and loveliness of heavenly objects to be easily elated or long satisfied with worldly prosperity.[11] They consider the temptations and dangers accompanying it, as well as the obligations and responsibilities that it occasions, and they feel the motives, which are thereby furnished, to humility and self-abasement. They consider themselves as stewards of God, to whose care much has been committed, and from whom, therefore, much will be required.[12]

2. Prosperity excites the love and gratitude of the saints to God, the author of their mercies. While it inflames the sinner's lusts, it fills the good man's heart with benevolent and grateful affections. Not that these outward things are the primary reasons or motives of his love to God; far from it: he loves him when he takes them away, as well as when he bestows them. But God sanctifies prosperity to his people and makes it conducive to their spiritual

---

11. "In such a temper of mind, the pomps and vanities of life are cast behind us as the baubles of children. We lose our relish for the frolics of gaiety, the race of ambition, or the grosser gratifications of voluptuousness. In the case even of those objects, which may more justly claim the attention of reasonable and immortal beings, in our family arrangements, in our plans of life, in our schemes of business, we become, without relinquishing the path of duty, more moderate in pursuit, and more indifferent about the issue. Here also we learn to correct the world's false estimate of things, and to 'look through the shallowness of earthly grandeur;' to venerate what is truly excellent and noble."—William Wilberforce, *Real Christianity* (1797).

12. Luke 12:48.

welfare, and subservient to their usefulness in the world.

3. The smiles of Providence usually render holy men increasingly watchful against sin. They reflect thus: 'Has God favored and prospered me? Then I am under the greater obligation to obey and please him.' They cannot sin, because grace has abounded, just as they would not dare to sin, that grace might abound.

4. A child of God will not be satisfied with all the prosperity and outward comforts in the world as his portion. When Providence became more than ordinary bountiful in temporal things, Luther became anxious, and earnestly protested against being put off course by them.[13] A lukewarm self-deceiver, however, will eagerly take earthly things for his chief good. If his selfish endeavors are not frustrated, and if he can make sure of the world, he will easily forget God, and leave heaven and hell at hazard. But the Lord is ever the portion of the saints; they have chosen him for their eternal inheritance and no earthly thing can occupy his place in their affections.[14]

---

13. "Remove vanity and lies far from me: give me neither poverty nor riches; feed me with food convenient for me: lest I be full and deny you, and say, 'Who is the Lord?' Or lest I be poor and steal, and take the name of my God in vain."—Proverb 30:8-9.

14. "The Lord is my portion, says my soul; therefore will I hope in him."—Lamentations 3:24.

CHAPTER 5
Trials of Adversity on Men's Hearts

CHAPTER 5
Trials of Adversity on Men's Hearts

No one who has either studied the Scriptures or observed human experience can doubt that adversity is adapted to try men's hearts. When the dross of corruption and the rust of hypocrisy, had nearly eaten out the heart of religion among the Jews, God said, *"I will melt them and try them;"*[1] accordingly they were cast into the furnace of affliction and tried.

Prosperity multiplies those who profess faith, but adversity brings them to such a test, that the precious are separated from the vile.[2] Job was tried by adversity and although some dross was

---

1. Jeremiah 9:7.

2. "Many profess Christianity, not because the means of grace warm the heart, or that they see any excellency in the way of God above the world, but merely to follow the fashion." "Religion in credit makes many professors, but few proselytes; but when religion suffers, then its confessors are no more than its converts, for custom makes the former, but conscience the latter. He that is a professor of religion merely for custom-sake, when it prospers, will never be a martyr, for Christ's sake, when religion suffers. He that owns the truth, to live upon that, will disown it, when it comes to live upon him."—Matthew Mead, *The Almost Christian Discovered or the False Professor Tried and Cast.*

discovered, he came forth as gold. Adversity brings out to view, not only the hypocrisy and corruption of the wicked, but also the sincerity and holiness of the righteous; it manifests the faith and patience of the saints.

In discussing this topic, it will be necessary to inquire what effects are common to both the sound and the unsound, and what effects are peculiar to each, in the trial of adversity.

Effects of Adversity Common to All

The following particulars relating to adversity, may apply to both saints and sinners.

1. Both may entertain fears of adversity when they perceive its approach. While impending judgments cause the sinners in Zion to tremble and fill the hypocrites with fearfulness, saints also, though for different reasons, may be agitated with concern and apprehension.

2. When the cup of affliction comes, the holy as well as the sinful, may receive it with reluctance. The wicked will indeed, ever loath and resent it; and, although it is accompanied by a thousand mitigations to the righteous, they also may shrink from it.

3. Troubles, disappointments, and pain may sometimes produce impatience in saints, as well as in sinners. Flesh and blood can hardly endure anguish and privation with composure. But if in

such circumstances grace is not always so powerful in God's people, as to overcome the propensity to be disquieted, it will still restrain them from such indulgences as the wicked allow.

4. The ungodly as well as the godly may be driven to their closets and their knees by adversity—the former perhaps for the first time, the latter with increased punctuality and engagement.

I need not detail the different motives of saints and sinners when in similar conditions; their external appearance and conduct is in some respects alike. I therefore pass on to those things that are peculiar to each.

Effects of Adversity on the Unsanctified

In the first place, let us consider the discoveries that are made by adversity of the hearts of unsanctified men.

1. An unsanctified man is not easily made to recognize and acknowledge the hand of God, in the calamities and troubles that befall him. He is prone to refer them to some natural cause, or to suppress the idea of any producer of them, or to credit them to the malice or negligence of men.[3] Thus, the creature bounds his horizon and contrives to secure his conscience from alarm.

---

3. This is indeed true; however, there are also those who will acknowledge God's providential hand in their troubles and even those who will go so far as to accuse him of thereby committing an evil or injustice against them.

2. Unsanctified men are not apt, in seasons of adversity, to retire into their closets, to search their hearts, to ascertain what they have done, to repent of their wickedness, and submit themselves to God. Afflictions rarely lead them to self-examination; they do not choose to think that they have done anything to occasion their troubles.

3. A man destitute of real faith, if left to his own choice, would prefer sin to affliction, and consider sin the lesser evil. He can contemplate the defilement of his soul with composure, rather than suffer the loss of his goods, his pleasures, or his present ease; and thus, the unsoundness of his heart is revealed. The saints on the contrary, will never knowingly consent to the commission of sin, even if it might prevent ever so much personal suffering or loss.[4]

4. Unregenerate men in adversity will turn from creature to creature, in pursuit of comfort and relief, instead of leaving all creatures and repairing to God for support; and when all their creature comforts fail, they sink in despondency.

5. An unsanctified man never comes out of the furnace of affliction purified, humbled, and made better than when he was cast into it; the fire does not consume his dross; the more he is afflicted, the

---

4. "Not only the guilt, but the love of sin, and its dominion, are taken away, subdued by grace, and cordially renounced by the believing pardoned sinner."—John Newton, *The Lamb of God, the great Atonement.*

worse he becomes. The reason is plain: afflictions themselves cannot purify men's souls, and those, which come upon the wicked, are not sanctified to them. Think on this, you who have had numberless afflictions of one kind or another, but have derived no benefit from any of them.

Effects of Adversity on the Sanctified

I suppose the reader may now desire to know what effects adversity usually has upon sincere humble Christians, but before I proceed, let it be observed that saints realize these effects, not so much while their trial continues, as after it has past, when they have opportunity for calm reflection. The fruits of sanctified affliction are lasting and they affect the Christian's whole temper and deportment. Still, some particulars may be mentioned, which apply to all.

1. Every real Christian, in time of affliction and adversity, will make God his refuge and look to him for comfort and relief. *"I found,"* says David, *"sorrow and trouble, then I called upon the name of the Lord."*[5]

2. The people of God particularly recognize his providence in all their adversities and troubles, whatever instruments may intervene. And this apprehension of the divine agency is fundamental to that communion with God, which saints in

5. Psalm 116:3-4.

affliction maintain; and to the holy submission and heavenly composure, which they feel.[6]

3. Christians are heartily disposed to justify God in the severest afflictions that come upon them, as well as in all his other dealings. The proofs of this in Scripture are so numerous, that it would be superfluous to quote them.[7] They may receive treatment from men, which they are conscious they do not deserve, but if God should add condemnation to affliction, they would vindicate not only his character and government, but also his dispensations to them.[8]

---

6. "In the covenant of grace, God has engaged himself to keep you from the evils, snares, and the temptations of this world; in the covenant of grace, God has engaged himself to purge away your sins, to brighten and increase your graces, to crucify your hearts to the world, and to prepare you and preserve you to his heavenly kingdom. Consider also that by afflictions he effects all this according to his covenant: 'If his children forsake my law, and walk not in my commandments; if they break my statutes, and keep not my commandments, (then will I visit their transgression with the rod, and their iniquity with stripes. Nevertheless my lovingkindness will I not utterly take from him, nor suffer my faithfulness to fail.' Ps. 89:30-34.)"—Thomas Brooks, *The Mute Christian under the Smarting Rod (2011 Hail & Fire Edition).*

7. "Then Job arose, and tore his mantle, and shaved his head, and fell down upon the ground, and worshipped, and said, 'Naked I came out of my mother's womb and naked shall I return: the Lord gave, and the Lord has taken away; blessed be the name of the Lord. In all this Job did not sin, nor charged God foolishly."—Job 1:20-22.

8. "The afflicted soul knows that a righteous God can do nothing but that which is righteous; it knows that God is not to be controlled, and therefore, the afflicted man puts his mouth

4. Good men in adversity examine themselves and endeavor to ascertain why they are afflicted; to find out what they have done or neglected, on account of which God contends with them. Their prayer is, *"That which I do not see, teach me; show me if there is any evil way in me."*

5. Every real Christian deliberately chooses to continue in adversity, rather than to be delivered from it by any sinful means. Christians are not insensible to pain, but rather than sin against God, they can cheerfully submit to disappointments, privations, and sufferings.[9]

6. The people of God do not fail to bless him for sanctified afflictions; esteeming the happy effects of them on their own minds, more highly than deliverance from them. If their affections are weaned from this world, if their sinful propensities are mortified, if they are advanced in the divine life, and made more meet for heaven, by means of adversity, they never think it too great or too long continued.[10]

---

in the dust and keeps silence before him."—Thomas Brooks, *The Mute Christian under the Smarting Rod (2011 Hail & Fire Edition).*

9. Daniel 3:13-18 | Hebrews 11:24-27.

10. "Before I was afflicted, I went astray: but now have I kept your Word. You are good, and do good; teach me your statutes."—Psalm 119:67-68 | "When we are afflicted, it is because there is a need-be for it. He does it not willingly. Our trials are either salutary medicines, or honorable appointments, to put us in such circumstances as may best qualify us to show forth his praise."—John Newton, *The Works of John Newton.*

CHAPTER 6

*Discovering the State of the Heart
through its View of Sin*

CHAPTER 6
Discovering the State of the Heart through its View of Sin

Nothing more thoroughly discloses the real state of men's hearts, than the manner in which they regard indwelling sin, or the practice of sin; herein is their soundness or their corruption exposed.[1] This topic, therefore, deserves a careful and ample elucidation.

Several considerations pertaining to the views and feelings entertained by holy and sinful men, respecting the practice of sin and sin in the heart, must be mentioned, in order to manifest who are

1. "Let us appeal to a test to which we resorted in a former instance. *'Out of the abundance of the heart ... the mouth speaks.'* Take these persons then in some well-selected hour, and lead the conversation to the subject of religion. The utmost that can be effected is to bring them to talk of things in the gross. They appear lost in generalities; there is nothing precise and determinate, nothing that implies a mind used to the contemplation of this object. In vain you strive to bring them to speak on that topic, which one might expect to be ever uppermost in the hearts of redeemed sinners. They elude all your endeavors; and if you make mention of it yourself, it is received with no very cordial welcome at least, if not with unequivocal disgust; it is at the best a forced and formal discussion."—William Wilberforce, *Real Christianity*.

the children of God and who are of the wicked one. By considering the different reasons for which saints and sinners abstain from the indulgence and commission of sin, we shall see the contrariety between their two characters and may perhaps ascertain to which class we ourselves belong.

Reasons the Ungodly Abstain from Sin

1. A false professor or unrenewed man may abstain from some sins because they are inconsistent with the committing of other sins. Thus hypocrisy and profaneness, prodigality and covetousness, are opposed to one another, so that only one can reign at a time.

2. An unsanctified man may be hindered from committing some sins by the restraint of divine Providence. It often happens, when men have conceived a sin and are ready to execute it, that they are unexpectedly prevented. And through these interventions of Providence, by which the designs of the wicked are overthrown, the world is saved from numberless, if not from infinite evils.

3. A wicked man may abstain from some sins, merely because committing them is inconsistent with his constitutional make[2] or repugnant to his health. Thus, some men cannot be drunkards, even if they would; others cannot be covetous and base.

---

2. Constitutional make: that is, the natural disposition or frame of one's mind or body, whether bred in or inherent.

4. Men totally destitute of moral goodness may be deterred from committing many sins by the force of education, the principles of morality, the authority of superiors, or the influence of popular opinion.

5. Such men may abstain from many sins through fear of their temporal consequences. Thus, they may avoid such sins as are punishable by human laws, and such as are followed by infamy and detestation among men. Some even look further to the punishment of sin hereafter; though they are not afraid to sin, they are afraid to burn for sin.

These are some of the reasons why ungodly men sometimes refrain from committing some sins.

Reasons the Godly Abstain from Sin

The reasons, upon which the saints abstain from indulging sin in their hearts and from committing sin outwardly, are such as manifest them to be children of God.

1. A primary reason why they abstain from sins of every kind, is that all sin is in opposition to that being whom they love supremely and who is worthy of all love and obedience. The love of God, which is shed abroad in their hearts, renders the indulgence of sinful feelings and actions peculiarly painful to them and, so far as this love prevails, it is an effectual restraint.

2. The saints cherish a holy fear of God, which renders the indulgence of sin exceedingly odious

and repugnant to them, and operates as a universal restraint. This fear exists wherever holy love and adoring reverence are exercised towards the supreme being, and good men are as much moved by it in secret as in public. It keeps alive the reflection that the eye of Omniscience is upon them.[3]

3. Saints feel a settled aversion to the indulgence of sin, on account of its evil and injurious nature, its polluting and debasing influence, and its horrible effects. They have an abhorrence of sin on its own account, and this greatly restrains them from sinful thoughts and feelings, as well as actions.[4]

4. The people of God abstain from sin, because it is repugnant to the holy principles by which they are moved and contrary to the pious habits, which it is their happiness to cultivate. They find their enjoyment in the performance of duty and feel the influence of a thousand motives to constancy in the discharge of it. The indulgence of iniquity, in heart or life, fills them with regret and misery; it wounds their own souls, obstructs their peace,

---

3. "The eyes of the Lord are in every place, beholding the evil and the good."—Proverb 15:3.

4. "Sin is the burden under which he groans; and he would account nothing short of a deliverance from it worthy the name of salvation. A principal part of his evidence that he is a believer arises from that abhorrence of sin that he habitually feels. It is true, sin still dwells in him; but he loathes and resists it: upon this account he is in a state of continual warfare; if he was not so, he could not have the witness in himself that he is born of God."—John Newton, *On Blindness.*

and dishonors the cause in which their present and eternal interests are involved.

5. It is the nature of that repentance which characterizes the saints, to turn them from sin in every form. They hate and abhor sin for its own sake, for its nature, for its intrinsic evil; they loathe themselves on account of it; they are filled with holy sorrow, with ingenuous self-condemnation, abasement, and regret, in view of it, as committed against God.[5] Thus, those who have felt the workings of genuine repentance, are, as it were, impelled to abstain from every kind of disobedience.

6. The children of God remember that the blessed Jesus suffered the death of the cross on account of sin: *'therefore, the love of Christ constrains them, for they thus judge, that if one died for all, then were all dead, and, that he died for all, that they who live should not henceforth live unto themselves, but unto him who died for them and rose again. Their old man is crucified with him, that the body of sin might be destroyed, so that henceforth they should not serve sin.'*[6]

Reasons the Ungodly Sometimes Hate Sin

The character of saints and sinners, respectively, is manifested by their hatred of sin. A few particulars will suffice to show why the wicked sometimes hate sin.

—————————————— •

5. "I abhor myself, and repent in dust and ashes."—Job 42:6.

6. 2 Corinthians 5:14-15 and Romans 6:6.

1. Although an unholy man will not hate sin for its own sake or as it exists in himself, yet he may exercise a kind of hatred towards it as exhibited in others. Thus, a proud man may hate the appearance of pride in his neighbor. He that has a beam in his own eye, a grossly corrupt heart, or depraved practice, may be quick to espy a mote in another's eye, some comparatively venial fault, and be swelled with disgust and aversion on account of it.[7]

2. A wicked man may hate sin as a criminal may hate the gallows, for its effects. Its guilt, its intrinsic evil, excites no concern, but its connection with hell is frightful and odious. The unsound professor sometimes wishes that there were no threatenings in the Bible against sin. When sin entices, 'I would,' he says, 'but I fear the consequences; could I but separate you from perdition, I would gladly comply.'

3. That hatred of sin, which sinners may sometimes feel, from various motives, is not habitual and permanent; it is not such as greatly weakens their love of iniquity in themselves, or their approbation of it in the general practice of the world.

---

7. "For with what judgment you judge, you shall be judged: and with what measure you use, it shall be measured to you again. And why do you behold the mote that is in your brother's eye, but not consider the beam that is in your own eye? Or how will you say to your brother, 'Let me pull the mote out of your eye,' and behold, a beam is in your own eye? You hypocrite, first cast the beam out of your own eye; and then you shall see clearly to cast out the mote of your brother's eye."—Matthew 7:2-5.

Reasons the Godly Hate Sin

The people of God hate sin for entirely different reasons, and their hatred is of an opposite nature.

1. They hate sin because it is evil in itself, because it is opposed to the supreme being and to all goodness, and ruinous in its influence and effects. Its evil and odious nature excites hatred and opposition, wherever the love of holiness exists.[8]

2. They hate sin in themselves, more than as exhibited by others; for they are more affected by the consciousness of their own sins, than by the consideration of those which they perceive in their neighbors.

3. They hate not this and that sin merely, but sins of every description, all sin; and to this, no hypocrite, self-deceiver, or unregenerate man can ever pretend.

4. They hate sin with an irreconcilable aversion; nothing could induce them to regard it as they once did. They have begun to oppose it, and will never cease to abhor it and contend against it, until this warfare shall cease to be necessary.

5. Their hatred of it is supreme; they hate it as the root and essence of all evil; their aversion to it is equaled, in strength, only by their love of holiness.

---

8. "The fear of the Lord is to hate evil."—Proverb 8:13.

6. Such is their detestation of sin, that they gladly cherish the thoughts of death, as the means of their deliverance from it with all its odious and defiling accompaniments.

Reasons the Ungodly Sometimes Sorrow for Sin

The troubles and sorrows, which men have on account of sin, reveal who has genuine, and who false faith. All concern on account of sin does not imply sincerity or true religion; some have reason to be alarmed in view of their concern itself.

1. Such are they who are troubled when they have committed some gross sins that startle the natural conscience, but who are not filled with anxiety, sorrow, and penitence, for secret sins, for sins of thought, for sins that defile the soul, for all sin.

2. They undoubtedly have graceless hearts, who are distressed at the discovery of their sins by others, but who are not troubled on account of their guilt. Multitudes there are of this class: they are not awed by the consideration that God sees them; they are chiefly concerned that their appearance before men may be reputable; they scruple not to commit ten sins against God, in order to hide one from the eyes of men.

3. An unholy man may be greatly distressed with the sufferings or embarrassments that his sins have brought upon him, while he does not regard the sins themselves.

Reasons the Godly Sorrow for Sin

On the contrary, however, the distress and anxiety of the saints, on account of sin, are of another kind, and imply a very different character.

1. They are troubled because God is dishonored, because his holy law is violated, and the interests of his kingdom disregarded or opposed.

2. They are troubled because sin defiles and debases their souls; renders them unfit for the presence and enjoyment of a holy God; and interrupts their love of purity.

3. Sin brings trouble and sorrow to the people of God, by occasioning the withdrawal of his gracious presence, and obstructing their communion with him.

4. Their distress and anguish on account of sin, is far greater and far more piercing, than other men feel; they can bear other troubles, while they nearly sink under those occasioned by sin.

5. They give vent to the sorrow and misery that they feel on account of sin, in secret, rather than in the presence of even their most intimate acquaintance. Indeed, they can hardly express what they feel to mortals, but God knows their hearts, and to him they can unbosom themselves without embarrassment or fear of misapprehension.

6. They never obtain relief from these troubles by such means as unsanctified men employ; they

apply for help to the Physician of souls, and are relieved only when they obtain pardon, submission, and peace.

Power of Sin in the Godly & Ungodly

Let us now consider the difference between saints and sinners, in regard to their subjection to the dominion of sin. The scriptures plainly teach us, that the wicked willingly yield themselves to the reigning power of sin, and that the righteous do not. In order to judge correctly of our own character, it will be necessary to show what may be common to them both, in relation to this subject; what distinguishes those who are under the dominion of sin; and what is peculiar to those who have been freed from the bondage of sin and death.

1. Both saints and sinners may be guilty of gross and scandalous offences; but we cannot thereby infer that sin reigns in one as well as in the other. None are free from the workings of indwelling sin; which may sometimes hurry good men into uncommon acts of wickedness, but which the wicked willingly and habitually indulge.[9]

---

9. "Every appearance of hypocrisy does not prove the person who manifests it to be a hypocrite. You should carefully distinguish between the appearance and the predominance of hypocrisy. There are remains of deceitfulness in the best hearts; this was exemplified in David and Peter; but the prevailing frame of their hearts being upright, they were not denominated hypocrites for their conduct."—John Flavel, *Keeping the Heart.*

2. Nor does it follow that both are under the dominion of sin, from the mere fact that they are repeatedly guilty of the same acts of wickedness, though such repetition on the part of one who professes faith, tends greatly to bring his sincerity into question.[10]

3. Though a saint, under certain circumstances, may be impatient of reproof for sin as the wicked are, yet from that alone it cannot safely be concluded that he, like them, is under the power of sin.

4. If some particular sin has more power than another in a good man as well as in sinners, it is not therefore certain that he is as much under the dominion of that sin as they are.

5. Though both good and bad men commit sins against knowledge, it will not thence follow, that such sins reign in the former as they do in the latter.

Dominion of Sin in the Ungodly

I proceed to note some things by which the dominion of sin is implied.

1. The dominion of sin consists in its prevailing sway over men, and their voluntary subjection to it; hence, deliberate consent to acts of wickedness, or to sinful thoughts and feelings, proves that

---

10. "Dead flies cause the ointment of the perfumer to send forth a stinking odor: so does a little folly him that is reputed for wisdom and honor."—Ecclesiastes 10:1.

sin reigns in the heart. Good men do not thus consent, though they may every day commit sin, and sometimes through the violence of temptation fall into gross iniquity.

2. The habitual practice of sin shows its dominion over the heart.

3. Delight in the ways of iniquity, imply the uncontrolled authority of sin, and a willing subjection to it: hence, it is said of the servants of sin, that, *"they have chosen their own ways, and their soul delights in their abominations."*[11]

4. Impatience of Christ's government and service, weariness of serious exercises and pious habits, and love of amusement, indicate a heart subject to the dominion of sin.

Dominion of Righteousness in the Godly

There remain to be considered some particulars, to show that the saints are not in subjection to sin as the wicked are.

1. If they fall into sin, they cannot reflect on it without shame and sorrow: but the wicked either derive satisfaction from the review of their sinful indulgences, or with stupid insensibility dismiss them from their recollection.[12]

---

11. Isaiah 66:3.

12. "When (man) cannot any longer deny that he is guilty of sin, he says that it was only a very little one. And it is long before you can get him to admit that sin is exceedingly sinful;

2. When the people of God fall into one sin, they are greatly excited by that, to guard against the commission of others. Not so with the servants of sin; the more they practice iniquity the more their inclination to sin is strengthened.

3. It is the prevailing desire and earnest prayer of the saints, to be in every respect freed from sin—from the love, the influence, and the practice of it.[13] On the contrary, those who serve sin consider their bondage to be liberty; they love their lusts and would esteem deliverance from them a hardship.

4. The saints pray for nothing more frequently or more ardently, than to be kept from committing sin. They implore nothing more earnestly than the assistance of God's grace, to fortify them against temptations. They have scarcely any occasions of more lively gratitude and joy, than are furnished by those interventions of Providence, which prevent their falling into sin. They use their own best endeavors to avoid the occasions of sin, they are restless and unhappy when they have gone astray, and they have comfort and peace only when piously engaged in the discharge of some duty. From all this, it is evident that they are not under the dominion of sin, and do not allowedly practice it.

indeed, no human power can ever produce genuine conviction in the heart of a single sinner; it must be the work of the Holy Spirit."—Charles H. Spurgeon, *Lectures to My Students.*

13. "Blessed are they that hunger and thirst after righteousness: for they shall be filled."—Matthew 5:6.

Opposition to Sin in the Godly & Ungodly

There remains to be considered, one particular with reference to the manner in which men regard sin; it is their opposition to it, whether in heart or practice.

1. There is both a universal, and a particular opposition to sin; the former is maintained by the regenerate, while the latter may be exerted by unregenerate men. As the saints hate, so they oppose every false way;[14] and they must necessarily do so, for they hate and oppose sin on its own account, because it is sin. With them, therefore, there can be no reservation, no favorite lust that will not, with sin in every form, meet their aversion and resistance.

But on the contrary, if unsanctified men, whether hypocrites, carnal professors, or self-deceivers, make any opposition to open immoralities, they will yet reserve and cherish their own secret sins, their favorite lusts, and their accustomed forms of iniquity; for they are not opposed to sin as such, but rather to its disgraceful or fatal effects.

2. The opposition of the saints to sin, is founded not merely nor chiefly in the consciences, but in their hearts; whereas if wicked men discountenance sin from anything other than worldly motives, their dislike arises so entirely from the remonstrances of

---

14. Psalm 119:104 and 128.

conscience, that their hearts will, at the same time, love and defend it as earnestly as ever.

There is an irreconcilable enmity and aversion between a holy heart and all sin; therefore, the reason, the conscience, and the affections of good men are opposed to it. Contrariwise, sin is the very element of unholy hearts, the wicked love its ways, and if their consciences oppose it, they hate their consciences rather than the thing opposed.

3. Sin is habitually and perpetually opposed by the people of God; they have waged a war of extermination against it, and while the enemy is unsubdued, will never cease to contend. The partial opposition of sinners, however, is unsteady and transient, being remitted and renewed as interest, caprice, or slavish fear directs.

4. They who are sanctified, oppose the root as well as the branches, the existence as well as the influence and effects of sin; but the wicked are concerned only to prevent its unhappy consequences.

5. The saints, in the strength of the Lord and the power of his might, exert themselves to oppose sin; but the ungodly trust in an arm of flesh, in the strength of their resolutions or the security of their self-righteousness; the weapons, which they employ in this warfare, are not spiritual but carnal, and therefore impotent and futile.[15]

---

15. 2 Corinthians 10:4-5.

6. Such is the opposition made by the saints against sin that their unholy propensities are subdued, their sanctification is promoted, and their progress in the divine life accelerated. The wicked, however, gain no advantage by their feeble and inconstant proceedings against sin—they may, in their own way, pray and hear, vow and resolve, but when all is done, they are still the servants of sin, their corruptions are unsubdued, and their hearts devoid of holiness.

CHAPTER 7
Discovering the State of the Heart through the Performance of Religious Duties

CHAPTER 7
Discovering the State of the Heart through the Performance of Religious Duties

Men's hearts are tried and revealed by the manner in which they perform the duties of religion. The following observations will illustrate this and show the difference between saints and sinners—between those who perform their religious duties acceptably and those who do not.

1. The designs and desires of men, when they attempt to discharge their religious duties, show what they are at heart. The designs and expectations of hypocrites, self-deceivers, and other unsanctified men, are ever low and contracted; adapted to answer their worldly ends or merely to quiet their conscience. Those of God's people, on the contrary, are liberal and elevated, suited to glorify God and procure important blessings to themselves.

2. The objects that occupy men's hearts, when they attempt to engage in the duties of religion, will lead to a discovery of their character. Those who are destitute of real holiness take little heed to their hearts, being comparatively indifferent whether they

are wholly unaffected or employed upon earthly objects. It is the earnest wish and endeavor of the saints, however, to have their hearts fully occupied with divine things, to have their attention fixed, their affections elevated, and their motives pure.[1]

3. The conscientiousness of men in the discharge of their private, as well as public duties must not be overlooked in estimating their characters. Unsanctified men may be driven by their consciences to the closet and the sanctuary, but they are not conscientious either in statedly repairing to them or in performing their appropriate duties. A thousand worldly motives may indeed influence them to affect religion in public, but the same will not allure them into retirement for the purposes of piety. And to a scrupulous attention to either public or private duties of religion, from such motives as the Gospel inculcates, they are utter strangers.

The saints on the contrary, not only cannot long subsist if they neglect a conscientious discharge of these duties, but are inclined to practice them in a holy manner and from holy motives. It is the nature of true religion to induce a scrupulous and constant attention to these various duties, especially such as belong to the closet and such as relate to positive

---

1. "Give me understanding, and I shall keep your law; yes, I shall observe it with my whole heart. Make me to go in the path of your commandments; for therein do I delight. Incline my heart to your testimonies, and not to covetousness. Turn away my eyes from beholding vanity; and quicken me in your way."—Psalm 119:34-37.

institutions: real Christians find their happiness in the performance of duty.[2]

4. If we would know whether men are Christians, or mere pretenders to faith in Christ, we must inquire whether they are assiduous and persevering in the practice of piety. They, whose faith is false, may at times make a show of engagedness and zeal: when danger threatens, they may pray vehemently; when religion is popular, they may be amongst the foremost to countenance it; but let danger disappear and their praying will cease, let persecution arise and they will leave those to endure it who love religion for its own sake; for they attend to the forms of religion, only when impelled by slavish-fear, allured by deception, or incited by worldly interest.

True religion on the contrary, affords a permanent foundation in the saints, and furnishes powerful motives for assiduous constancy in the discharge of the various duties of piety. Whether dangers are apprehended or not, whether religion is popular or otherwise, whether their worldly interests are promoted or retarded by it, whether it procures favor or reproach, the saints will be holy still. They embraced religion for reasons that can be little

2. "It is the nature of true grace, that however it loves Christian society in its place, yet it in a peculiar manner delights in retirement and secret converse with God. So that if persons appear greatly engaged in social religion, and but little in the religion of the closet, and are often highly affected when with others, and but little moved when they have none but God and Christ to converse with, it looks very darkly upon their religion."—Jonathan Edwards, *Religious Affections* (1746).

affected by such things as these; they counted the cost and are not disappointed. They have gained by religion what they can never lose, and they still find in it sufficient to render the happiness it confers, and the exercise of the duties it enjoins, their highest privilege and glory. They love religion now and choose *"always to abound in the work of the Lord."* The ways of piety are to them ways of pleasantness, and all her paths are peace; they joyfully anticipate the entrance for which they are preparing to the world above, where they will be free from the obstructions, which here surround them, and where religion will fully and eternally employ all their powers.[3]

---

3. "Almost all that is said in the New Testament, of men's watching, giving earnest heed to themselves, running the race that is set before them, striving and agonizing, wrestling not with flesh and blood, but with principalities and powers, fighting, putting on the whole armor of God, and standing, having done all to stand, pressing forward, reaching forth, continuing instant in prayer, crying to God day and night; I say, almost all that is said in the New Testament of these things, is spoken of and directed to the saints." "But doubtless there are some hypocrites, that have only false affections, who will think they are able to stand this trial; and will readily say, that they desire not to rest satisfied with past attainments, but to be pressing forward, they do desire more, they long after God and Christ, and desire more holiness and do seek it. But the truth is, their desires are not properly the desires of appetite after holiness, for its own sake, or for the moral excellency and holy sweetness that is in it; but only for by-ends. They long after clearer discoveries that they may be better satisfied about the state of their souls; or because in great discoveries self is gratified, in being made so much of by God, and so much exalted above others; they long to taste the love of God, (as they call it) more than to have more love to God. Or,

5. The humility and self-denial of men's hearts when engaged in duty, is closely connected with their true character. He, who has Christian humility and self-denial, will exercise it, especially when he approaches the presence of Almighty God. It will occasion in him the most reverential apprehensions of the Divine Majesty, the deepest self-abasement, the most hearty renunciation of all dependence on himself or his own doings, and an entire reliance on the blessed Mediator for acceptance.

6. Another consideration by which men's hearts may be tried is whether in the discharge of duty they have communion with God.

It is beyond contradiction, that unsanctified men never have communion with God, they never have what in Scripture is so termed; and it is undeniable, that the saints do realize what is meant by this phrase, when they are engaged in the exercises of religion. This holy fellowship or communion, is founded in real union to the Lord Jesus Christ; it is enjoyed by those who have been brought nigh to God by reconciliation, and who draw near to him in duty; and if it cannot be adequately described

---

it may be they have a kind of forced, fancied, or made longings; because they think they must long for more grace, otherwise it will be a dark sign upon them. But such things as these are far different from the natural, and as it were, necessary appetite and thirsting of the new man, after God and holiness. There is an inward burning desire that a saint has after holiness, as natural to the new creature as vital heat is to the body."—Jonathan Edwards, *Religious Affections* (1746).

to others, its reality, its present effects, and its blessedness are known to the people of God.

Let it be observed, that if some of these remarks, like such considerations as respect the spirituality of saints, and their growth in grace, are true of some in a higher degree than of others, yet their universal application is safe, and they are as definite as the case requires.

CHAPTER 8
Trials of Suffering for Faith & Religion

CHAPTER 8
Trials of Suffering for Faith & Religion

We are come to the last class of trials proposed for consideration; let us attend to it with seriousness and self-application. Thousands embark on the profession of faith in a calm, who, when the winds rise and the sea rages, and they see a storm gathering that threatens destruction unless their carnal goods are thrown overboard, and their worldly expectations abandoned, forget the destined port, and desire to be landed, as soon as may be, upon the shore whence they departed. Thousands rank themselves with the company of the saints, who, when tribulation or persecution arise, turn back and herd again with their own kind.

But since every degree of suffering for religion's sake, is not sufficient to cause a separation of the vile from among the precious, I shall show what trials of this nature may be deemed sufficient; why such must necessarily discover who has false faith; and what advantages true holiness has to endure them.

Trials that Separate True Christians from False

The following instances are selected, as being sufficiently severe to separate the dross from the gold, the false from the true believer.

1. When the dearest interests of men, related to this world, their earthly lives, liberties, or fortunes, are placed in imminent hazard because of religion, few, except the genuine children of God, will maintain their steadfastness and glory in the loss of all things—rather than dishonor the name by which they are called, and incur the guilt of allowing anything to compete in their affections with the glory of God and their own eternal interests. In cases like this, false hearts will show themselves.

2. When there remain no hopes of deliverance from such trials, or any visible encouragement that the scene will vary, then the hands of the false-hearted hang down, and their hearts faint.

3. When an unsanctified man is subjected to sufferings, alone, it is a thousand to one but he quits religion to save himself. Good company may encourage the irresolute and false-hearted, but they will faint and fail if called to sustain the fight single-handed; they lack those inward and invisible supports, which uphold the saints in such circumstances.

4. When powerful temptations are combined with sufferings, with the desertion of friends and the opposition of relatives, then hypocrites and

self-deceivers will leave religion and heaven to be maintained and enjoyed by the saints.

Why these Trials Separate True Christians from False

That these trials will distinguish true Christians from mere pretenders may easily be made evident.

1. During such trials, the predominant interest and attachment of men will be made manifest. No man can serve two masters whose injunctions clash with each other; he will, in ordinary times, secretly hold to the one and despise the other, but when his obedience and fidelity are put to the test, he will openly show whom he truly serves.[1] In these trials, the two great interests of men, this world and heaven, the flesh and Christ, stand opposed; one must be adhered to, the other abandoned. Christ says, *'Be faithful unto death; he that loves father or mother, wife or children, lands or inheritance, bodily ease, temporal safety, or life itself, more than me, is not worthy of me.'*[2] The flesh says, 'Spare yourself; he that will grieve and break the hearts of these dear relatives, forsake these earthly accommodations, exchange ease for sufferings, and hazard life, is not worthy of them.' Those, therefore, who love Christ supremely, will follow him wherever he

---

1. Matthew 6:24 and Luke 16:13.

2. Matthew 10:37-39.

leads, while the unholy will cleave to the world and to the flesh.[3]

2. When brought to suffer for the kingdom of heaven's sake, the saints derive their supports, not from any visible or sensible objects, which would be utterly insufficient, but from an invisible source, from their covenant God, their Savior, their Sanctifier. This method of preservation, only the saints have, and therefore, only they can live through such trials.

3. In such times, men's notions and speculations about religion, their visionary hopes and self-comforting imaginations, vanish away, and those only who are rooted and grounded in the truth, will be likely to remain steadfast.

4. These trials reach the foundations of men's faith and hope, and will demolish such as are laid in the sand, while such only as are built upon the Rock of Ages, will abide their vehemence and pressure.[4]

---

3. "He that takes up religion only to serve a turn, will take no more of it than he imagines will serve that turn; but he that takes up religion for its own excellent and lovely nature, takes up all that has that nature—he that embraces religion for its own sake, embraces the whole of religion. This shows why gracious affections will cause men to practice religion perseveringly and at all times."—Jonathan Edwards, *Religious Affections* (1746).

4. "The holy Scriptures do abundantly place sincerity and soundness in religion, in making a full choice of God as our only Lord and portion, forsaking all for him, and in a full determination of the will for God and Christ, on counting the cost; in our hearts closing and complying with the religion of Jesus Christ, with all that belongs to it; embracing it with all

Advantages of True Holiness in Suffering

I proceed to show the advantages of true holiness, when sufferings on account of faith are to be endured.

1. Holiness takes the throne in the hearts of God's people and destroys the dominion of selfishness; supreme love to God predominates and renders those interests, which have the supreme regard of sinners, subordinate. Thus, they love that for which they suffer, while their sufferings tend to subdue propensities and attachments to which they are opposed.[5]

2. By true holiness, the affections of the saints are placed on heavenly and divine objects, they become heirs to an eternal and glorious inheritance, and are disposed to look, not at things which are seen and temporal, but at those which are unseen and eternal; hence they esteem the sufferings and tribulations with which they meet in the way to heaven, as light

---

its difficulties; as it were, hating our dearest earthly enjoyments, and even our own lives, for Christ; giving up ourselves, with all that we have, wholly and forever, unto Christ, without keeping back anything, or making any reserve; or, in one word, in the great duty of self-denial for Christ, as it were, disowning and renouncing ourselves for him, making ourselves nothing that he may be all."—Jonathan Edwards, *Religious Affections* (1746).

5. The saints' affections are drawn heavenward in suffering for the Gospel's sake; such trials purify and refine them, and fan their spiritual graces to a blaze. It is not so with false Christians, whose chief interests lay in this world and whose hearts cleave to its passing pleasures and bodily comforts.

and unworthy to be compared with the end they have in view.[6]

3. By holiness, man's will is brought into a cordial subjection to the will of God and, in the exercise of Christian submission, the saints can patiently endure whatever sufferings, trials or privations are allotted to them.

4. Holiness has all good beings and all goodness on its side; it has the support of the Redeemer's intercession, the prayers of the saints, the assistances of the Holy Spirit, the promises of God's Word: therefore, *'neither tribulation, nor distress, nor persecution, nor famine, nor peril, nor sword,'* shall be able to separate the saints from the love of Christ, or terminate their obedience to him.[7]

---

6. "Yet the inward man is renewed day by day. For our light affliction, which is but for a moment, works for us a far more exceeding and eternal weight of glory; while we look not at the things which are seen, but at the things which are not seen: for the things which are seen are temporal; but the things which are not seen are eternal."—2 Corinthians 4:16-18 | "I reckon that the sufferings of this present time are not worthy to be compared with the glory which shall be revealed in us."—Romans 8:18. See also, Colossians 3:1-4 and Hebrews 11:1.

7. Romans 8:35.

CHAPTER 9

God's Purpose in Appointing Trials
for His People

CHAPTER 9
God's Purpose in Appointing Trials
for His People

Some of the ways in which God brings the holiness of his people to the touchstone, in this world, have been mentioned, and illustrated—the design of these trials is now to be considered. Without doubt, we may conclude, in general, that God designs to promote his own glory and the good of his people; both of which will certainly be accomplished. But for our improvement, a more particular exhibition of the ends answered through these events, is necessary.

Benefits Arising from Trials

If we take a close look at this subject, we shall perceive many important benefits arising from these trials of the sincerity and holiness of God's people.

1. Hypocrisy is unmasked, the vizard[1] is plucked from the false professor, and his real character is displayed to the world. Should any object, that this produces evil instead of good, that many are

---

1. Mask.

stumbled and hardened by it, and that the world observes its mischievous effects—I answer, that some are, indeed, thus prejudiced and rendered obdurate, so as never afterwards to think well of the government and people of God, but who does not see that his Word and his purposes are thus accomplished? And if these stumble, fall, and perish, yet others will be warned, awakened, and put to searching their own hearts; and hence good will arise, for *they who think they stand, will take heed lest they fall.*[2] Again, by such disclosures of the corruption and danger of hypocrites and false professors of faith, they, themselves, have better opportunities and greater advantages than they ever had before, to escape from the snare of the devil. Their refuges of lies are swept away, their illusions and pretenses are dissipated, and they are rendered more accessible to truth and more open to the convictions of conscience.

2. By these trials, the uprightness of the saints is manifested, their doubts are resolved, and their fears allayed. What would not many Christians give, what would they not suffer, what would they not gladly perform, if they might attain satisfaction in these respects! How many tears have they shed in secret, how many hours have they spent in the examination of their hearts, without being able to

---

2. 1 Corinthians 10:12 | It might also be noted that hereby the church is relieved of certain deceptive and sinful influences, as various heresies, legalisms, libertinisms, false teachings, false divisions, and confusions typically accompany the professions of false Christians, in one variety or another.

accomplish this object? But they find, at last, that trials are the high road to assurance; they have been cast into the furnace, and have come forth as gold purified in the fire. Their holiness has been put to the test and its reality demonstrated, not only to themselves, but also to the world, which may now look upon the heavenly face of sincerity and truth, and see that true religion has the luster and loveliness of immortal glory.[3]

3. These trials are eminently calculated to subdue and destroy the remaining pride and self-confidence of the saints; who thus become more intimately acquainted with their hearts, and learn to detest what is evil and to cherish what is good.

4. By trials, stupidity and slothfulness are prevented, and grace is kept in exercise. Even the best men are apt, unless often visited by some trial, to slacken in their diligence and lose much of their fervor in religion.

5. When the graces of the saints are tried, Satan is put to shame, and his malicious insinuations confuted. It is not uncommon for the devil and wicked men to charge the people of God with hypocrisy, and to persuade the world that they are not what they pretend to be; these suggestions and

---

3. "It is God's manner, in his Providence, to bring trials on his professing friends and servants, designedly, that he may manifest them, and may exhibit sufficient matter of conviction of the state which they are in, to their own consciences, and oftentimes to the world; as appears by innumerable Scriptures."—Jonathan Edwards, *Religious Affections* (1746).

calumnies[4] are overthrown by such trials as have been considered.

6. These trials exhibit living testimony against the infidelity of the world; they demonstrate that faith is no fancy, as the thoughtless and sensual would esteem it; that the ardency of its professors is not blind bigotry and mistaken zeal; and that its doctrines and duties are not without efficacy, nor its effects destitute of high and lasting importance.[5]

---

4. Calumnies: that is, slanders and false accusations.

5. "Experience warrants, and reason justifies and explains the assertion that persecution generally tends to quicken the vigor and extend the prevalence of the opinions, which the world would eradicate. For the peace of mankind, it has grown at length almost into an axiom, that 'her devilish engine back recoils upon herself.' Christianity especially has always thrived under persecution. At such a season, she has no lukewarm professors; no adherents concerning whom it is doubtful to what party they belong. The Christian is then reminded at every turn, that his Master's kingdom is not of this world. When all on earth wears a black and threatening aspect, he looks up to heaven for consolation, he learns practically to consider himself as a pilgrim and stranger. He then cleaves to fundamentals and examines well his foundation, as at the hour of death. But, when religion is in a state of external quiet and prosperity, the opposite of all this naturally takes place. The soldiers of the church militant then forget that they are in a state of warfare. Their ardor slackens, their zeal languishes. Like a colony long settled in a strange country, they are gradually assimilated in features, and demeanor, and language, to the native inhabitants, till at length almost every vestige of peculiarity dies away."—William Wilberforce, *Real Christianity* (1797).

CHAPTER 10
Only True Holiness Endures these Trials

CHAPTER 10
Only True Holiness Endures these Trials

Such only is true holiness, as will bear these trials. Before I confirm this truth, I will first endeavor to prevent some mistakes, which a misapprehension of it might occasion.

1. We ought not to think because we are to be in a state of trial throughout life, and know not how we shall appear after future trials, that therefore assurance of our gracious state is unattainable. Such a conclusion cannot be fairly drawn from the position that I am to confirm. Instead of indulging any such speculations, let Christians be grateful for the mercies that they have experienced hitherto, and trust in God for all the assistances of which they may hereafter stand in need.

2. Nor should it be imagined, that any saint has so much holiness as to be able, if left to himself, to sustain these trials, though not one saint will by any means be overcome by them. Saints are not distinguished, one from another, in this respect; all are, at all times, equally dependent on the gracious influences of the Spirit of God.

I now proceed to confirm the proposed truth, and to show, that such seeming grace as has never been tried or will not bear trial, ought not to pass for genuine, as it will neither comfort men now nor fit them for heaven at last.

1. All is not gold that glitters: great numbers of persons in the professing Christian world are deceived and destroyed by trusting to apparent, but untried grace. They cannot determine that they have true holiness unless some trial is made of it and if a trial is made that they cannot endure, the conclusion must be against them; hence they grope in uncertainty and stumble at last where neither deliverance nor mitigation can reach them. Such was the miserable condition, and such, probably, was the fate of the Laodiceans mentioned in the text. They imagined themselves rich, but were in truth, poor and wretched; their fancied gold had never been tried in the fire. Reader, do not pass over this topic without some serious reflection in regard to your own spiritual state.

2. The promises of salvation are made to such holiness, such faith, such religion, as will endure trial: *"Blessed is the man that endures temptation; for when he is tried, he shall receive the crown of life, which God has promised to those that love him."*[1]

Not to him who sets out in the morning with resolve and gallantry, but to him who holds out to the evening of life, does the promise apply, *"He*

---

1. James 1:12.

that endures to the end shall be saved."[2] Hence if any who have sustained slight troubles, shall afterwards faint and fail under severe trials, all their labors and their hopes will prove vain.

3. Every man's character must be scrutinized at the final judgment, and if those who pretend to faith in Christ, cannot endure the trials to which they are now exposed, how can they bear the investigation to which they will then be subjected? Surely if we have not such holiness as will bear the severest tests to which it can be brought in this life, we can hardly hope that it will sustain the ordeal of the last day.[3]

4. True holiness is willing to be tried; true saints greatly desire to know their condition, and choose to be searched and proved. But false religion strives to avoid the touchstone, and shrinks from scrutiny.[4]

---

2. Matthew 24:13.

3. "I saw a great white throne, and him that sat on it, from whose face the earth and the heaven fled away; and there was found no place for them. And I saw the dead, small, and great, stand before God; and the books were opened: and another book was opened, which is the book of life: and the dead were judged out of those things which were written in the books, according to their works."—Revelation 20:11-12.

4. "This is the condemnation, that light is come into the world, and men loved darkness rather than light, because their deeds were evil. For everyone that does evil hates the light, neither comes to the light, lest his deeds should be reproved. But he that does truth comes to the light, that his deeds may be made manifest, that they are wrought in God."—John 3:19-21.

Saints wish to know the truth respecting themselves, whatever it may be, and no matter how difficult its attainment. Those who prefer that their supposed grace should not be tried are secretly conscious of its falseness, and of their insincerity.[5] Reader, I do not know your case, but if your heart is in any measure right in the sight of God, you will desire to know the worst of yourself. After making the most thorough trial of which you are capable, you will be disposed to submit to the scrutiny of Him who cannot err: if such is not your case, you have but too much reason to class yourself among the rejected Laodiceans.

---

5. "I will tell you what small, weak, little grace will do, and not do, in opposition to common grace. It will not oppose much grace; the least spark of fire will not oppose the flame, or resist the flame. Water will, however, because fire and water are contrary: and so, false grace will oppose the highest degree of grace, saying, 'Why need you be so strict and precise? You may go to heaven with less ado.' But the least degree of true grace will not oppose the highest; for it loves examination, it loves to examine, and to be examined; for it is sincere, and sincerity is much in examination." "It holds up all its actions to the sun and light; it loves the work of examination. False, counterfeit, common grace does not do this."—William Bridge, *A Lifting Up for the Downcast* (1648).

CHAPTER 11

Trials Will & Must Come—Examine
Yourselves

CHAPTER 11

Trials Will & Must Come—Examine Yourselves

Now I shall offer some inferences from the subject and some persuasions to self-examination.

Offences Must Come

1. If what has been said regarding the trials of the holiness of the saints is correct, then let none who hope for salvation, think to pass through this life in quietness, exempt from this searching experience.[1] You may please yourselves with the ideal felicity of living at ease, but it is the delusion of hell, and if God loves you, he will in some way most certainly try and prove you: such has ever been the economy of his dealings with those whom he delights to honor, and who at last, being purified as gold, shall inherit his kingdom.

2. In view of what has been said, be guarded against too much confidence of your good state: your period of trial has not expired; *"you have not*

---

1. "Yes, and all who desire to live godly in Christ Jesus will be persecuted."—2 Timothy 3:12.

resisted unto blood striving against sin; be not high minded but fear."[2]

3. If true holiness must be tried in this world, as gold is tried in the fire, then it greatly concerns all men, at their setting out, to build upon the sure foundation, and to anticipate severe and repeated trials. If any have not done this, it behooves them to do it now. I warn you, reader, to count the cost before you attempt to build. To the test you must come and by truth you must be judged; if you hope to endure to the end, you must have the spirit of a martyr.

4. It may be observed in view of this subject, that scandals and offences, in connection with religion, are unavoidable. *"It is necessary that offences come,"*[3] for all who are exposed to trials will not be able to bear them; some therefore will be offended. But the holy God will accomplish his ends, both in them that are saved and in them that perish.

On the whole, true saints have abundant reason to be encouraged. But hypocrites and self-deceivers

---

2. Hebrews 12:4 | "Many persons, as was formerly hinted, are misled by the favorable opinions entertained of them by others; many, it is to be feared, mistake a hot zeal for orthodoxy, for a cordial acceptance of the great truths of the Gospel; and almost all of us, at one time or another, are more or less misled by confounding the suggestions of the understanding with the impulses of the will, the assent which our judgment gives to religious and moral truths, with a hearty belief and approbation of them."—William Wilberforce, *Real Christianity* (1797).

3. Matthew 18:7.

would do well to be dismayed, for if they are not exposed in this life, they are sure to be hereafter.[4]

Examine Yourselves, Prove Yourselves

If men must be tried as gold is tried in the fire, then it is of great importance that they should examine and prove themselves, and it cannot be unsuitable to urge this duty here.[5]

1. The difficulty of this work ought to excite you especially and resolutely to undertake it; since your welfare requires that it should be performed. If it were an easy thing to ascertain the real state of the heart, you might delay the investigation with more safety; but it has never been considered an easy task. Moreover, perhaps you, as well as others, may find a difficulty in two respects: in bringing your heart to the work, and in successfully conducting the examination. Do not defer it, therefore, if you would attain a well-founded peace, and avoid final shame and perdition.

2. The discovery of sincerity and holiness, after an honest and faithful examination, will abundantly reward you for your pains. I need not describe the

---

4. "For God shall bring every work into judgment, with every secret thing, whether it is good, or whether it is evil."—Ecclesiastes 12:14 | "Shall God not search this out? for he knows the secrets of the heart." Psalms 44:21.

5. "Examine yourselves, whether you are in the faith, prove your own selves. Do you not know your own selves, that Jesus Christ is in you, unless you are reprobates?"—2 Corinthians 13:5.

value and the blessedness of such a discovery; the experience of it alone, can be useful to you.

3. The vast interests of your souls in this matter ought to awaken you to the utmost diligence in examining yourselves. Your eternal happiness stands or falls with your sincerity; bring your hearts then to the trial. Your thoughts cannot be occupied on a more momentous subject; a portion of your time cannot be employed to better purpose; a business more worthy of your closest attention cannot be named.

4. Remember, that whether prepared or unprepared, whether saints or sinners, you must ere long stand before the judgment seat of Christ, and be approved or condemned.[6] Therefore examine and prove yourselves now, and be willing that God should try you as he pleases in this world, that confusion and woe may not overwhelm you at last.

---

6. "We must all appear before the judgment seat of Christ; that everyone may receive the things done in his body, according to what he has done, whether it be good or bad."—2 Corinthians 5:10.

CHAPTER 12

Discovering Sincerity &
Detecting Hypocrisy

CHAPTER 12
Discovering Sincerity &
Detecting Hypocrisy

Now to propose various helps for discovering sincerity and detecting hypocrisy.

Discovering Sincerity

I shall venture here to offer some observations that may assist in the discovery of sincerity.

First: every real reason of humiliation on account of sin is not a proper cause of doubt, whether we have genuine holiness or not.[1] It is the unhappiness and the sin of some good souls, to construe everything unfavorably towards themselves; they do not judge candidly and therefore cannot expect the comforts which piety confers on others.[2]

Second: the doubts and fears that we indulge concerning the unsoundness of our hearts do not

---

1. "For there is not a just man on earth that does good and does not sin."—Ecclesiastes 7:20.

2. "Why read over the evidences of God's love to your soul, as a man does a book that he intends to confute? Why do you study evasions, and turn off those comforts which are due to you?"—John Flavel, *Keeping the Heart*.

prove that we are destitute of holiness. Saints, who are free from doubts and fears, are rarely to be met with.[3]

Third: let him who would ascertain the state of his heart, examine it impartially, remembering, that for the smallest as well as for the greatest manifestations of sanctifying grace, God must be praised.

It may be advantageous to such, to occasionally ask themselves questions like the following:

> *Do I seek the approbation of God or the applause of men in my religious exercises?*

> *Is it the reproach and shame that attends sin at present or the misery that will follow it hereafter, or is it love to God and hatred of sin that restrains me from the commission of it?*

> *Do I heartily rejoice to see God's work carried on in the world, and his glory promoted by the instrumentality of others, although the honor and the benefits of it do not result to me?*

> *Is there no duty so difficult or self-denying, but I desire to perform it when required?*

---

3. "Real believers are always thinking they believe not, therefore they are fighting, wrestling, striving, and toiling without ceasing, to preserve and increase their faith. Just as good and skilful masters of any art are always seeing and observing that something is lacking in their work, whilst bunglers and pretenders persuade themselves that they lack nothing, but that all they make and do is quite perfect."—Martin Luther, *Watchwords for the Warfare of Life.*

Am I resolved to follow Christ and practice holiness at all times and in all events?

Am I rigidly conscientious in abstaining from secret sins and in performing secret duties?

Such questions proposed in a calm and serious hour can hardly fail to reach the heart.

Detecting Hypocrisy

As the upright and sincere are apt to apply to themselves the characteristics of hypocrites or self-deceivers, so these on the contrary, are eager to appropriate to themselves the graces and expectations of saints. Some remarks must therefore be made to discover their ruinous mistakes.

First: it is not enough to clear a man from self-deception, that he does not know himself to be deceived. Doubtless, many are deceived and will finally perish, who are not now sensible of their state, because they have never seriously examined it and ascertained the truth.

Second: a man may be deceived himself, though he hates hypocrisy in another, and though he shows great zeal in the cause of God; these, and similar dispositions may arise from different motives of the worst kind.

Third: the reputation that a man's piety may have gained among Christians will by no means prove that he does not deceive himself—he may have a name to live while dead. Nor will the respect that he may show to the servants of God avail, for this may spring from selfish and unholy motives.[4]

Let such persons press these and similar questions upon their consciences:

When I attempt to perform any duties towards God, do I engage my heart in them?

Am I not influenced by self-interest, worldly advantage, reputation, or ease, in my religious proceedings?

Have I not made such reserves as are inconsistent with the obligations of a Christian?

By what am I deterred from the committing of sin?

How is my conscience regarded in reference to secret sins and duties?

Some Last Words of Advice

I have only to add some advise to such as may read this treatise.

First: let it be your great object to have a holy heart, a renewed and right spirit. All the helps and

---

4. "Nothing can be certainly concluded concerning the nature of the religious affections that any are the subjects of, from this, that the outward manifestations of them and the relation persons give of them, are very affecting and pleasing to the truly godly, and such as greatly gain their charity and win their hearts. The true saints have not such a spirit of discerning that they can positively determine, who are godly, and who are not: for though they know experimentally what true religion is, in the internal

directions in the world will not preserve you from delusion and ruin, unless your heart is sanctified.

Second: make religion the business of every day; let it regulate all your conduct, and engross your affections. Consider well the motives of your actions; maintain a constant watch over your propensities; and especially when visited by sickness or trouble, give vigilant heed to the admonitions of conscience.

Third: away with all temporizing in religion;[5] be an honest man, faithful to your Master and true to yourself. Do not live for this world, but for heaven. Keep your heart under the awe of God's presence and hourly pray,

"Let integrity and uprightness preserve me,
O Lord, for I wait on you."[6]

---

exercises of it, yet these are what they can neither feel, nor see, in the heart of another. There is nothing in others, that comes within their view, but outward manifestations and appearances; but the scripture plainly intimates that this way of judging what is in men, by outward appearances, is at best uncertain and liable to deceit (1 Samuel 16:7; Isaiah 11:3)."—Jonathan Edwards, *Religious Affections* (1746).

5. Temporizing in religion: that is, conforming religion to the culture and opinions of the time.

6. Psalm 25:21.

"The Scriptures are the touchstone.
If you would not have a counterfeit religion
deceiving you in the end, when you have
trusted to it, I pray you to test yours
by the Word of God."

Hugh Binning
1627-1653

"I beg you, take the Scriptures for the rule of your walking or else you will wander; the Scripture is *'regula regulans,'* a ruling rule. If you are not acquainted with it, you must follow the opinions or examples of other men, and what if they lead you to destruction?"

Hugh Binning
1627-1653

By purchasing **Hail & Fire paperbacks**, you help support our effort to acquire and convert rare and important Christian works into free online books, audio books, and paperback reprints and republications.

Thank you.

Hail & Fire
www.hailandfire.com

Other Paperbacks

Free Online Library

Keeping the Heart *by* John Flavel

The Forgiveness of Sin *by* John Owen

Christian Love *by* Hugh Binning

Religious Affections *by* Matthew Henry

Real Christianity *by* William Wilberforce

An Alarm to the Unconverted Sinners
by Joseph Alleine (Originally published 1672)

The Benefit of Christ's Death *by* Aonio Paleario
(Originally published 1543 in Italian)

Institutes of the Christian Religion
by John Calvin (1840 Edition in 2 Volumes)

The Truth of the Christian Religion
by Hugo Grotius (Originally published 1627)

The History of the Waldenses *by* Jean Paul
Perrin (Christian history, 1624 Edition)

**The Israel of the Alps; A Complete History of
the Vaudois of Piedmont** *by* Alexis Muston
(Christian history, 1857 Edition in 2 Volumes)

Important Considerations *or* **A Vindication
of Queen Elizabeth** *from the Charge of Unjust
Severity Towards Her Roman Catholic Subjects, by
Roman Catholics Themselves by* William Watson
(Originally published 1601)

& much more!

"The hail shall sweep away the refuge of lies."
Isaiah 28:17

Hail & Fire

Hail & Fire is a resource for Reformed and Gospel
Theology in the works, exhortations, prayers,
and apologetics of those who have
maintained the Gospel and
expounded upon the
Scripture
as the Eternal Word of God
and the sole authority in Christian doctrine.

For the edification of those who hold the Gospel
in truth and for the examination of every
conscience, Hail & Fire reprints
and republishes, in print
and online,
Christian,
Puritan, Reformed
and Protestant sermons and
exhortative works; Protestant and
Catholic polemical and apologetical works;
bibles, histories, martyrologies, and eschatological works.

Visit us online:
www.hailandfire.com